GOLDEN RULE LEADERSHIP

Gordon Ferguson
Wyndham Shaw

GOLDEN RULE LEADERSHIP

Building a spirit of team and family in the body of Christ

DPI
DISCIPLESHIP
PUBLICATIONS
INTERNATIONAL

Golden Rule Leadership
© 2001 by Discipleship Publications International
2 Sterling Road, Billerica, Mass. 01862-2595

Printed in the United States of America

ISBN: 1-57782-132-7

Cover Design: Tony Bonazzi
Interior Design: Corey Fisher & Tony Bonazzi

Note: An F at the beginning of a chapter indicates that Gordon Ferguson is the primary writer. An S indicates Wyndham Shaw.

From Gordon

To Blayze David Ferguson

As our latest grandchild to arrive, you are viewed as a
special bundle of love from heaven. You join brother, Bryce, and
cousin, Aleea, as unbelievably precious gifts from God to our family.
We pray that you will be led in your home and in the church with
the principles described in this book and that you will one day lead
others for God according to these same principles. May he grant that
your life be one of great impact on eternity in the same way that you
have already made such an impact on our hearts.
God bless you, my grandson!

From Wyndham

To my family who have most helped me to learn
Golden Rule leadership:

Jeanie—my true companion and giver of the most love
and forgiveness in my life
Melissa—our oldest child and great giver of love
and encouragement
Kevin—our first son-in-law and joyful addition to the family
Kristen—our beloved daughter and great example of
perseverance and insight
Samuel—our oldest son and source of great joy
and companionship
Jacob—our youngest son and my greatest inspiration to practice the
Golden Rule

Contents

Foreword

We in the International Churches of Christ are a part of a relatively new, dynamic spiritual movement with very lofty goals and ideals. We not only want to restore the standards of the Bible in God's church today, but we also want to be the church in this generation that Jesus Christ established on that incredible day of Pentecost (Acts 2). God has blessed this effort in unbelievable ways by allowing us to plant congregations of disciples in nearly every nation of the world. Places that were considered closed to the gospel a few years ago now have healthy, growing churches.

With this amazing growth, an increasing number of challenges have come. A new congregation, when it first is begun, is relatively problem free. Most of the initial group are mature, committed and single-minded disciples with a clear purpose: make other disciples. As the group grows in number, the obstacles to growth increase. The needs of the new Christians must be met. No longer is the group spiritually mature; now the baby Christians must be grounded in the faith. Their life issues must be dealt with. Weak marriages must be strengthened, often with hours of counseling. Benevolent needs must be met. With growth often comes persecution. And with more people, more meetings are needed to keep everyone involved and united. The whole growth process is very similar to the maturing of our own physical families. For example, life for young married couples is very simple, but it certainly grows more complex as they go from parents of the first baby, to several toddlers, to early school years and on through the teen years.

Of course, the answer to meeting the challenges of the maturing church lies in its leadership. Often the small church planting is led by a young, dynamic couple who is full of zeal, but short on experience. The group is enthusiastic and forgiving of shortcomings in the couple's leadership. However, as the group grows, not only must the couple mature in their leadership skills, but they must also raise up and train an ever-increasing number of new leaders. I believe this is the single greatest barrier to our continued growth as a movement.

Gordon Ferguson and Wyndham Shaw have tackled this problem head-on in *Golden Rule Leadership*. They haven't just aimed at the target, but they have hit a bull's eye. Both Wyndham and Gordon are elders and leaders in the great Boston Church of Christ, a church of more than 4,000 members, with a weekly attendance of 7,000 (October 2001). I have worked side by side with both of them and count them among my best friends. Their greatest credentials are their families, for this is the ultimate proof of a man's leadership. Their book is not based on some ideas that they think might work. They have been on the front lines of leadership for more than two decades and have learned valuable lessons through prayer and searching the Scriptures, through trial and error, through the school of hard knocks.

I wholeheartedly recommend this exciting new book to every leader and to every aspiring leader in God's kingdom. If we all put Golden Rule leadership into practice, the church will continue to grow and mature for many, many years to come.

Al Baird
November 2001

Looking Ahead

Looking ahead is good. We need to look ahead in planning how to accomplish what God wants to do through us and with us and in us during the years ahead. Recently, Randy and Kay McKean, the world sector leader couple for New England/Continental Europe, took their discipleship group on our semiannual retreat. The beginning lesson, on which everything else was based, asked the question, "Where will we be ten years from now?" Randy began by reviewing the events of the previous decade to illustrate how we as the church have grown and the progress we have made. Thinking ahead to the next ten years led us into the reflective thinking that we all badly need: When you get where you're going, where will you be? Looking ahead is vital.

As a movement of God, we have just completed a six-year plan, which resulted in 402 churches in 171 nations. Without looking and planning ahead, most of this would not have happened. The only things that seem to just happen are dust, weeds and inertia! But where do we go from here? No doubt we will have a multitude of other plans in many forms, all designed to further evangelize the world in our generation. These will be good and are certainly needed, but the plans must take into account the ongoing need for healthy, probing and at times painful examination, especially of our leadership style and practices. No group succeeds—or survives—without a growing leadership. This growth must include many new leaders being raised up and trained, as well as each existing leader continuing to grow in significant ways. Once any person or group becomes satisfied with the status quo, the insidious process of decay sets in.

Leadership can be evaluated in many ways, and each way will have benefits. As elders, Wyndham Shaw and I feel that the maturity attained by both age and experience provides a very needed perspective on leadership. I have been a congregational elder in the Boston church since 1989, and Wyndham, one of my best friends and spiritual cohorts of all time, has served in this role since 1992. Both of us have spent years leading many types and sizes of ministry groups. Each of our perspectives has been broadened in other ways also, mine as a kingdom teacher and Wyndham's as a HOPE Worldwide geographical leader for our world sector. Both of us feel blessed to work with Randy McKean as our world sector leader and feel that our leadership team provides a very good example for others. In all honesty, it took years to forge this team into what it is today, and such forging cannot be done without plenty of heat. Nothing truly great in leadership ever comes quickly or easily, and this is true in our case as well. We will be sharing with you how our relationships were forged and are functioning in a fashion that brings increasing joy to each of us.

Before proceeding further, however, we must make one other point regarding our leadership team in Boston. We do not claim that we are a perfect example or that we have everything figured out—far from it. To be perfectly candid, we have found it more than a little challenging to keep the church growing numerically at a rate that we are pleased with and that we think God is pleased with. The growth rate is slowing in almost all of the larger American churches, and we think that it will keep slowing without some paradigm shifts in our leadership style. Boston is simply the oldest church among us and has hit walls earlier, especially in combination with the impact of having sent out hundreds of leaders to plant fifty-three churches all over the world. These factors have forced us to look for answers. It has taken us longer to make needed leadership changes than it should have, but even at that, we are further down the road in making needed changes than many younger churches are. We believe that you can learn from our experience, although we too are certainly a work in progress.

Wyndham and I wanted to collaborate on this book because together we form a very tight leadership team and because we understand the strengths and weaknesses that both of us bring to the table. We dispense lots of advice, but we probably ask for more advice than almost anyone else I know—from each other, from Randy and from Dan Bathon, our world sector administrator. Advice is needed and sought from others outside our circle, knowing we will have blind spots in our own leadership. I have emphasized the need to establish a leadership team that one will work with day to day. The people whom we work with consistently will know us best. This "on site" team must live with and must deal with the challenges, sins and shortcomings of our own lives and ministries as no one else can or will. The four of us in Boston need each other, and we know that we need each other.

Of course, as men need men, so also women need women in close relationship to provide input and encouragement. And, on top of this, we find great strength and great wisdom as we lead together and work together with our wives. Certainly the great women leaders throughout the kingdom help the men see and anticipate needs that without them we may miss. A great team is produced as we pray with, laugh with, cry with, struggle with and work with them in team leadership.

This book ardently holds up the team model of leadership, for it is our conviction that the lack of such is a root of many of our weaknesses in many churches. Neither of us would be comfortable writing a book about leadership individually, not only for fear that the content would be one-sided or incomplete, but also because of the example we wish to be of leadership functioning as a team.

Having said this, we must quickly add that the subject of leadership is far too broad for any one book to exhaust. Our goal in writing is to describe what we are calling "Golden Rule leadership" from the perspective of elders, shepherds of God's flock. Both of us also served as evangelists for years, leading churches and ministry groups of various sizes. In chapter 7, we will discuss the different perspectives that evangelists and elders have in focusing on short-range and long-range issues for building the church. Both types of leaders must keep in mind both sets of issues, but by design, evangelists are more focused on the short-range needs (moving the ministry in evangelistic outreach) and elders more on the long-range needs (keeping the saved, saved). With this in mind, the book is written to cover in some depth those issues that we believe will produce health and vitality in individual disciples, as well as in our ministry groups. Again, we are not trying to be exhaustive in treating the subject—that would be exhausting to both us and you! Did not Solomon warn, "Of making many books there is no end, and much study wearies the body"? (Ecclesiastes 12:12). We aim to provide some insight into key needs of leadership at this time in our history and to provoke all of us to think more purposefully and to discuss more honestly the things that we need to change and improve.

So, who should read this book? Actually, at some point, every disciple. Why? For two basic reasons: First, all of us lead in one way or another—as a parent, a husband, a discipler, a teacher in the children's ministry or as a group leader. And if we are imitators of Jesus, who was the world's greatest leader, we should aspire to lead in every way commensurate with our spiritual gifts from God. Second, in the church, leaders are like the parents of the group, and in keeping with that analogy, all the children need to know something about their parents' relational dynamics. Children who have little or no idea about these dynamics are unquestionably going to be very insecure. As long as they know how leadership in the home functions, assuming that it functions effectively, they will be fine. Similarly, God's children need to know how their spiritual parents function. Therefore, we are convinced that all disciples will benefit greatly from reading this book. The better you know another person, the greater the potential for close relationships. The better all disciples understand the design of leadership under which they function, the more they will love the church.

Looking ahead to the need of the hour, our prayer is that you will read and meditate upon each chapter carefully. We pray that God will use this book in the ways that we envision it should be used and further, that he will use it in ways we cannot now anticipate. By his grace and mercy we offer this book and wait in anticipation to see how his people, especially current leaders, will be helped by it. And to God be the glory!

WARNING!

The greatest mistake you can make in reading this book is to assume that you really already understand the principles being discussed and are currently putting them into practice. This is a great danger especially for our most experienced leaders. We do not see ourselves as we are; we do not see ourselves as others see us. Our strong tendency is to think more highly of ourselves as leaders than we ought to think (Romans 12:3). Here is my strong suggestion for current leaders: *have other leaders under your charge read the book and then discuss each chapter together*. Begin by asking them to honestly evaluate your strengths and weaknesses in each area being discussed. Better yet, ask another mature leader into your group to lead the discussion, who as a neutral facilitator can draw out what people really think about your leadership. Those around you have learned to praise you, but most likely they have not learned to evaluate you. (I wonder why?) Without this kind of pointed evaluation, you are going to continue believing that you are further along than you are.

God has blessed our movement in amazing ways. There are great leaders who are leading us in their examples of courage, faith, sacrifice and love. There are also weaknesses and sins in all of us. God has often used us in spite of our leadership weaknesses. However, I am convinced that he is calling us higher and will not continue to bless us in spite of our weaknesses if we are not doggedly determined to painfully examine them—and to keep growing and changing. Therefore, we are challenging you to act on what we have long said is the cardinal rule of discipleship: Assume nothing. Please do not assume that you are effectively doing what we discuss in the book. Evaluate—or better yet, volunteer to be evaluated by others. The result will be beneficial beyond your wildest expectations—guaranteed!

Okay, now you can proceed to chapter one! Let us take this most urgent of subjects very seriously. God is serious about it: "Not many of you should presume to be teachers, my brothers, because you know that we who teach will be judged more strictly" (James 3:1). Thanks and God bless.

Golden Rule Leadership

F

> NOTE: If you have not yet read the introduction carefully, please go back and read it before proceeding. Pay special attention to the section entitled "Warning!" near the end.

In its simplest form, what we call the Golden Rule is stated in Luke 6:31 in these words: "Do to others as you would have them do to you." While we focus on this principle, it is helpful to picture Jesus walking in our own personal steps and contemplating our decisions. What would Jesus do? Righteous leadership could be described as leading others as you would like to be led or as Jesus would lead.

However, another mental picture touches my heart. Recently in a discipleship group, Chip Mitchell, who oversees the campus ministries in our world sector, described his concerns for his little boy. He was thinking ahead to the time when his little boy would be eighteen years old and entering college as a young disciple. In essence, Chip said, "My boy is going to be in the hands of young campus interns like the ones I now disciple. Just how will they treat him?" This is a good observation and an understandable concern. For me, Golden Rule leadership boils down to this: Treat God's children as you want your own children to be treated.

A word about family leadership style is apropos at this point. I remember hearing about a broad study of college students from different schools, relating their emotional well-being to the parenting style they had experienced growing up. It was quite telling and has direct correlation to leadership in God's family. In this study, four distinct parenting styles were discovered and defined:

the authoritarian (drill sergeant: do it my way with no back talk); authoritative (definitely in charge, but works through relationship); permissive; and indifferent. You will note in the following that the effectiveness of each was in direct proportion to the type and depth of relationship that it fostered.

The most effective style, not surprisingly, was the authoritative (Jesus' style). Second in effectiveness was the permissive. This style was not decisive enough, but at least it was relational in nature. Third in line was indifferent, a style without much relationship development at all, either good or bad. Dead last in effectiveness was the authoritarian style, which produced bad relationships and ultimately, rebellion. The scary part is the fact that the most effective and least effective styles (authoritative and authoritarian, respectively) share a number of characteristics in common. God's children will react to these leadership styles in much the same ways that physical children do. What is your leadership style? (You likely won't really know until you ask for enough honest input from those in your life at different levels.) This is an extremely important issue in leading like Jesus does. Please don't take it lightly.

Since Theresa and I have two children who are grown, with children of their own, we have some seasoned insights on the subject—not that we did everything right with our own children, for regrettably we did not. When we moved to Boston and were discipled in depth for the first time, Bryan was almost twenty and Renee was almost sixteen. Obviously, we had lots of catching up to do. Because of our mistakes as parents, Theresa and I went through a period when we second-guessed ourselves about how much we really knew about parenting. However, because of my confidence in the principles of discipling in general, I found myself feeling more and more confident about my understanding of parenting. Whether discipling God's children or our own children, most of the same principles apply. Theresa made a great observation about disciples who had been around

since the early days of our movement. Many who practiced discipling long before they had children had an excellent foundation for their parenting; but then later on, their parenting
revealed various weaknesses in their discipling. As they made
the changes in their parenting, they made adjustments in their
discipling of others as well. However, parents or not, all of us still
have a lot to learn about the subject.

Theresa and I have worked with a number of families in
which the children are reaching preteen and teen years and are
not doing well spiritually. (You really do not know how good a
job of parenting you have done until they are in and through
their teen years.) We have concluded that most parents follow
some discipling principles better with their children than they
do with God's children, but that the reverse is also true—some
follow vital principles better with other disciples than with their
own children. With all this in mind, consider the following four
key principles regarding the parallels between discipling your
own children and God's.

Principle One:
The Building of a Family Feeling Is Paramount

The New Testament has many descriptions and designations
for what we commonly call "the church," and each has special
meaning. Besides "church," God's people corporately are called
the kingdom, the body of Christ, a temple or building of God, a
field, the bride of Christ and the family of God. Interestingly,
some have a tendency to view the church in two other ways that
the Scripture does not develop: as an army, out to spiritually con-
quer the world, and as an athletic team. While it is true that
metaphors are used in connection with these two concepts, the
Bible does not specifically call the church an army or an athletic
team—which means that we need to handle these metaphors
with care. The athletic mind-set can play more into our worldly
pride and competitiveness than to the humility of the Spirit.

I think that the military perspective has deeper ramifications than we might think, making a significant impact on how we go about evangelizing the world. A nation's military branch actually deemphasizes relationships in order to insure the completion of the mission, no matter what the personal cost. Military leadership emphasizes "over/under" relationships instead of family ones. But the military is not a Spirit-driven organization and does not exist, as does the church, to specifically help the weak, the sick, the helpless and the lost. Fundamentally, every resource of an army is put toward capturing and conquering the enemy. Every resource of the church is designed to heal and to build. We are about building families that build villages that impact nations. We need to be very careful about how we view the church overall. The family analogy is the one most needed in guiding our thinking about Golden Rule leadership.

I suppose a family could be described as a team, a childcare unit, a guided study hall and more. But a family does not really feel like a family until the atmosphere at home is characterized by deep love, mutual respect and consistent gratitude between Mom, Dad and the children. Would not everyone agree with that? The church can be described as a kingdom, an army, a body, a farm, a vineyard, a temple or even a business. But can we not also agree that until a good family feeling predominates, it is not really the church God has in mind?

So, the relationships in the church should be like those in an ideal family. If it is not, two tragedies occur: (1) people leave and (2) people stay but are not fired up about helping their friends and physical families become disciples. Mark it down: The sense of being loved, appreciated, accepted and esteemed does more to draw people and hold people than anything we can think of. The greatest commands in the Word have to do with love. Love is greater than faith and greater than hope, and without it, nothing else really matters (1 Corinthians 13).

Who is responsible for building that family feeling? At the beginning of 1999, Randy and Kay McKean asked Theresa and me to move to Paris for several months for the express purpose of building family in the Paris church. Like many older congregations, the rate of those leaving was of great concern. One thing became obvious to us quickly. As mom and dad figures to the church, we could provide help and create some important memories, but we could not single-handedly bring about the family feeling that was so much needed. In a physical family, doing some unusual things that develop special family memories is essential, but the family atmosphere is much more the result of the day-to-day relationships within the home. Therefore, the leaders within the Paris church, especially those on the ministry staff, needed to feel responsible for developing the family feeling. With this in mind, read 1 Thessalonians 2:6-12 and meditate on its principles.

Knowing how to grow a ministry means much, much more than knowing ministry mechanics! Years ago, I began preaching for a church that had the ministry mechanics well in place (the organization was there to keep careful track of everything), but the leadership had been characterized by significant harshness. The atmosphere of the church was certainly not family in the sense the Bible discusses. It was much more like a typical dysfunctional family that too many of us experienced in the world. My focus as the new leader was simply to add in the dynamics of family, beginning with teaching the book of Romans (with its emphasis on grace). When this heart was added to the mechanics, the result was one of the most gratifying I had ever experienced before or since. Honestly, having lots of baptisms will mean little if those who are baptized do not remain faithful to God.

Building family is a leadership issue. Accomplish it, and your ministry will produce fruit that lasts; fail to accomplish it, and those going out the back door will be roughly equivalent in number to those who come into the baptistry. Our greatest contribution to the Paris church in the six months that we labored there was in helping the ministry staff learn to build team among themselves (Philippians 2:19-24, Colossians 4:7-8, Philemon 1:24) and family among the disciples. Go thou and do likewise.

Principle Two:
Disciple the Heart, Not the Behavior

A few years ago, a staff couple with young children asked me to tell them the one most important principle in childrearing. I told them that the answer to that one was easy: Disciple the heart, not simply the behavior. I believe that this is the most important principle in godly discipling, whether we are discussing training God's kids or our own. It is so tempting to focus on behavior rather than on what lies behind the behavior. I know of a situation in which a young, single person moved out of a Christian household while everyone else in the house was at a church activity—which meant that his leaving was premeditated. When the other disciples in the household learned of it, they said, "We just don't understand it. We thought he was doing fine." What does this reaction tell you? It should tell you that the heart of the one who left was not being discipled, although the behavior may well have been.

What do you think discipling the heart entails? Frankly, it involves much more than we assume. It is not simply a matter of opening the Bible and teaching people what is right. It surely is not a matter of just lecturing people and pointing out all their mistakes. Before the heart can be discipled, you must know exactly what is in it. How can you know? You can only know in depth when people open the curtain and let you into their hearts. When will people do this? Only when they are in a safe place where their fears of being honest are dispelled. Then and only then will people open up their hearts enough to really be discipled at the deepest level. Therefore, one of the most important functions of leadership is to create an atmosphere where love permeates to the point that fears are laid to rest. "There is no fear in love. But perfect love drives out fear, because fear has to do with punishment. The one who fears is not made perfect in love" (1 John 4:18).

Leader, please listen carefully and do not be quick to pat yourself on the back about how unintimidating you are. Because of their past experiences, many people come into the kingdom with negative views of authority. We did not create most of the problems that people have in fearing authority figures, but we must help them to develop healthy views through consistent, positive interactions with us. People in the world have been trained wrongly in about every area of life, and we now have the responsibility of training them to be spiritual. Embrace the opportunity, rather than resenting how they may initially view you and react to you as a leader. (This will take more love and patience than you may imagine right now.)

We must *want* people to be open with their true feelings. Need I state the obvious problem that many of us react to honesty incorrectly and shut people down? Instead of saying, "You shouldn't feel that way" or correcting them when their hurts are aimed at you, be grateful that they are trying to be open. They will likely start out by being open in a hurtful manner, but do not react to that. Help them to feel safe, and when they do, you can double back later and help them with their manner. Sure, they may come across in a prideful and hurtful way, but most likely they were never able to be honest with any authority figure in the world. Let them say what they need to say rather than going into a corrective mode. "You're just being prideful" is an ineffective response, in spite of its unfortunate popularity among many disciples. Openness is the goal, not perfection. If you handle honesty well, especially when it comes out with negative emotions, others will learn to express their hurts in a nonvenomous way. Be patient. Be quiet. Listen.

Asking the right kinds of questions is very helpful in facilitating openness, but the questions must be posed in a nonthreatening way. For example, asking "why" questions often puts people on the defensive. "Why did you…" makes the person feel like he or she is already on trial and probably guilty. Although this form of questioning may have been your parents' favorite, it is nonetheless not best. Try questions along these lines:

- What were you thinking when you made that decision?
- What exactly was going on when that happened?
- How did it turn out when you did that?
- In retrospect, how are you feeling about that now?

In addition to learning how to ask questions positively, learn to respond to negative statements positively. Instead of saying (verbally or nonverbally), "You did *what*?" learn to identify with others and put them at ease. For example:

- You think that's bad? I remember when I did…or thought….
- I remember feeling just about the same, and here's how I learned to look at it and feel about it.
- Others have said similar things, and here is another way to look at this….
- Thanks for being so honest. Let me mention a few things that have helped me [or others] in similar circumstances.

Help people understand that you too are human and have to struggle with your attitudes. Nothing dispels fear more than your own vulnerability and confession of sin. Just humble out and do it. Being a leader does not mean that you have become sinless. It means that you are learning how to deal with your sins Biblically, and you want to share with others how you are learning and growing. Be humble, you sinner, and you will become a real leader!

Once the heart is open and the true feelings come out, disciple the heart with faith and inspiration. After one of my relatives had become a disciple a few years back, he called me one day to tell me in despondent tones that he was struggling. Less experienced leaders would have been very sober or somber in tone as they warned him of the dangers of his struggle. My reply was different. I said, "You're struggling? Great!" In shock, he thought I had somehow missed completely what he had confessed. But I assured him that I had understood that he was struggling, but that I was encouraged by the struggle. A year earlier there would have been no struggle—he would just have given in to the sin. At least now he was fighting back! Before the conversation had ended, he was inspired to stay in the battle and win the victory. If such spiritual giants as Paul and Barnabas warned that "we must go through many hardships to enter the kingdom of God" (Acts 14:22), do not be surprised when it happens in someone's life. Respond with faith, not alarm and dismay.

The greatest tests we ever receive is when people are open with us about their critical attitudes toward us. It takes the greatest of self-control and love to avoid retaliation. Frankly, few leaders have learned to handle such "attacks" with grace. But the Bible could not be clearer about the necessity of doing so. My all-time favorite passage about communication in trying circumstances is 2 Timothy 2:23-26:

> Don't have anything to do with foolish and stupid arguments, because you know they produce quarrels. And the Lord's servant must not quarrel; instead, he must be kind to everyone, able to teach, not resentful. Those who oppose him he must gently instruct, in the hope that God will grant them repentance leading them to a knowledge of the truth, and that they will come to their senses and escape from the trap of the devil, who has taken them captive to do his will.

Engaging in arguments and quarrels is no more acceptable to God than engaging in sexual immorality or drunkenness—

each is forbidden. I recall a situation where a woman reacted emotionally to a verbal attack by another sister. When confronted with her failure to remain in control, she said, "Well, she made me mad!"—as if that somehow excused her response. Her defensiveness, despite her spiritual maturity and leadership responsibilities, reminded me that very, very few really understand what this passage is saying.

Continuing to be kind and to gently instruct someone who is out of his or her senses is not possible if we take things personally. This is what Paul was talking about when he wrote "not resentful"—simply meaning not to take what is said personally and reacting emotionally. We are to be more focused on the pain of the one lashing out than on our own feelings at that moment. Unless we learn to do this with our children, the preteen and teen years are going to be very challenging for us and for them. Some parents love their children enough to practice the principles of 2 Timothy 2 well, but do not love God's children enough to practice the same principles with them. I am not saying that this is easy, for it can be extremely difficult. But God says that it is a part of righteous leadership. When self jumps out, one thing is certain: self has not been crucified with Christ. No "buts" and no excuses—just obey God.

Principle Three:
Treat People Appropriately As They Age

Physical children do not respond well to being treated like five-year-olds when they are fifteen! In fact, they rebel. As they age, they must have increasing amounts of freedom with the additional choices that go with it. Raising children could be described as the process whereby you gradually replace your parent hat with a friend hat.

My father and I had a stormy relationship as I was growing up, but once I married at the ripe old age of twenty-two, everything changed. A part of the Ferguson culture evidently was that married children were independent adults and should be treated as such. The difference in our relationship was immediate and monumental. All of a sudden, he treated me with trust and respect, and we became the best of friends until his death twenty-seven years later. Although much of his parenting was off base, he had this concept down pat.

If we are strong, forceful leaders, we may be tempted to be too controlling with our children, and if we succumb to this temptation, the consequences can be disastrous. The scary part is that we may not discover the damage that we have caused until our children are out on their own—and perhaps not until they are in their late twenties or beyond. I am indebted to my father for taking off his parent hat and putting on his friend hat. I have imitated him and now marvel at the type of relationship I have with my grown children and their spouses.

In a parallel vein, spiritual children do not respond well to being treated like they are new campus converts when they are married leaders of their own families. Sometimes we hit the wall of ministry growth and think the wall is directly related to the size of the ministry and that growth just plateaus when we get to a certain point. I think it may be much more related to age than to size, because the two track together, don't they? Hopefully we have figured out that in our individual discipling we cannot simply lecture and give directives. However, with groups that we lead, we may not be applying what we have learned with individuals. Do we want to know what is in the hearts of disciples we lead and how they are really feeling about the things that we are asking them to do? Spiritually mature adults are tempted to rebel when they face two challenges: (1) when they are treated like new converts and (2) when they are made to feel like their age in the kingdom is a detriment instead of an advantage. Exasperated or sarcastic comments about their spiritual age only expose our true feelings toward them.

Unless they are treated with respect, older disciples are going to feel that they are not being treated fairly. Of course, it is easy to say that life is not fair, and in the world, this is definitely true. But the "fairness doctrine" in the church is essentially the Golden Rule. We as leaders can decide and do things that may have significant consequences in others' lives without really considering how to work *with* them in making those very decisions. We would be very unhappy if we were treated in the same way by our own leaders. Remember: "Do to others as you would have them do to you."

Principle Four:
Recognize the Need for Positive Reinforcement

Hopefully we have learned the power of building up our children. They are growing up in a negative world, and they take an emotional beating as a result. Certainly, we have to address negative behavior, but we cannot focus on these negatives. Everyone is made up of pluses and minuses, positives and negatives. When we say that we love someone, what do we mean? Do we mean only that we love the positives in them, or do we love them as a whole, warts and all? Good question, isn't it? We may be much more conditional in our love than we realize. Even when we learn to practice the fine art of unconditional love and acceptance of our own children, we do not necessarily follow the same path with God's children.

As leaders, we can easily develop a critical mode of evaluating others all the time and making them feel as if they never quite measure up, as if they never really please us (or God). This constitutes a form of conditional love and can be very damaging, especially as it relates to personal security and self-esteem. Our job as leaders is not simply to fix everything in everybody. It is to build an atmosphere of family acceptance that enables people to keep growing and changing out of appreciation for the unconditional love they are receiving. How do you tend to view people generally? Of course, those outside the kingdom are a mess. In the words of Titus 3:3 they are characterized by "being hated and hating one another." However, in the kingdom, it must be far different. In Romans 15:14, Paul wrote: "I myself am convinced, my brothers, that you yourselves are full of goodness, complete in knowledge and competent to instruct one another." Do you exercise this kind of love and trust, or do you have a suspicious air toward others in the church? Do you expect the best from them or the worst? Since your expectations come through the very pores of your skin, ask a number of people whom you lead exactly what they feel from you. It will likely be a real learning experience!

Love among disciples means that we always trust (1 Corinthians 13:7). The "us and them" mentality that often exists between the ministry staff and nonstaff is caused by a number of things, but our lack of trust (which may be quite subtle) is likely high up on the list. Children, physical and spiritual, usually rise or sink to our level of expectations for them as their leaders. With our own children, we can say that they are awesome and leave it at that, even knowing their downsides. Often with God's children, we say or think they are awesome, *but*... (followed by the negatives we see). The end result of this critical edge is that we come across as never quite satisfied, and this lack of acceptance takes a big toll on them. People who live under a critical eye suffer in myriad ways, including having a distorted view of themselves, God and God's family. Bending over backward to build others up is good exercise, and for many of us, it will take developing some new spiritual muscles. Try it; you may like it—and rest assured that those whom you lead will like it!

Giving positive reinforcement consistently and copiously demands that we accept and honor individual differences in those whom we lead. Children in our own families are going to be different from one another, often in remarkable ways. They will vary physically, temperamentally and in their personalities, abilities, interests and a plethora of other ways. Yet, we cannot measure them against ourselves or their siblings. An amazing amount of emotional damage has resulted from such comparisons, which may well have been made with the best of intentions. Each child is unique and of great value, regardless of the variations mentioned above. How well do we do in dealing with the differences among God's children? Of course, a reasonable degree of sameness is expected in order to preserve order. All children in a family need to come to the dinner table, and similarly, all of God's children need to come to church. But do we find ourselves holding up one type of disciple and being frustrated with another, rather than helping each to reach his or her God-given potential?

Paul said that the weaker parts of the body are indispensable (1 Corinthians 12:22). Is that really the way you feel? Figuring out when to have the same expectations of people and when to approach individuals in unique ways is a great challenge of leadership, but we must figure this out if we want people to feel like family. God's children want to know that they are loved as persons, not simply for their performance.

Do we love people? Do we love God's children like we love our own, and in both cases, are we following his principles in training them? These issues are the essence of what it means to build family. The Golden Rule of ministry is to treat God's children, not only the way you want to be treated, but just as you want your own children to be treated! Follow this principle and you cannot avoid being blessed greatly by God.

2

The Motivation Behind Leadership
Why Do We Do What We Do?

Purifying our motives in serving God and others is a life-time project. Truthfully, most of us have mixed motivations for doing good things. An in-depth study of our motivations can be very revealing and very unsettling at the same time. I find encouragement in the examples of Jesus' disciples and their misplaced ambitions because I see that Jesus kept his vision for them in spite of their sin—and they eventually changed. Misplaced ambition in leadership leads to a host of accompanying sins, with harsh treatment of those being led at the top of the list. Obviously, weaknesses like laziness and faithlessness in leaders also have serious consequences and must be repented of. However, harshness in leaders remains one of the most unsavory qualities imaginable. Two of Jesus' favorites, James and John, wanted to burn up an entire village (Luke 9:51-56), which by anyone's definition, brings the idea of harshness to an entirely new level! Jesus did rebuke them, but he did not kick them off the team—and John lived to be known as the great apostle of love.

Misplaced Ambition

I will say that harshness will either be repented of or Jesus will eventually take a harsh person out of leadership. I have seen him do it in a number of situations and have no doubt that he will always do it, in time. God sometimes chooses to use very unworthy vessels for a period to accomplish his will. But if this kindness on his part does not induce repentance on the part of the recipient (Romans 2:4), sterner measures will be forthcoming. If the insights gained in my own experience are accurate, there are at least two qualities that God will ultimately not tolerate in his leaders: unchecked pride and harshness. God seems to use leaders who have a number of weaknesses (thank you, Lord), but he will not keep using those who do not take their sins seriously by repenting and growing out of them.

Al Baird has recently been teaching about leadership from Matthew 20 and highlighting something that I somehow always overlooked in the passage. After the mother of James and John came with them to Jesus to request the leadership positions of honor (as they understood it), we find the following account:

> When the ten heard about this, they were indignant with the two brothers. Jesus called them together and said, "You know that the rulers of the Gentiles lord it over them, and their high officials exercise authority over them. Not so with you. Instead, whoever wants to become great among you must be your servant, and whoever wants to be first must be your slave—just as the Son of Man did not come to be served, but to serve, and to give his life as a ransom for many. (Matthew 20:24-28)

Several lessons must be learned from this passage. First, all the apostles were struggling with worldly views of leadership. The ten who heard about the request of the other two were indignant, not with righteous indignation over the sin of the two brothers, but with worldly indignation prompted by their own egotistical ambitions for those supposed seats of honor.

Second, not only is it wrong to lord it over those whom we lead, but it is wrong to exercise authority. This is precisely the point that Al made that I had previously overlooked. What does it mean to exercise authority? It means to appeal to it as a means of inducing people to submit to your leadership. For example, the Bible does teach that the husband is the head of the wife

(Ephesians 5:22-25). However, if the husband has to appeal to that authority, then he has already lost his case. Either his leadership influence brings about voluntary submission on the part of the wife, or he has lost his leadership—pure and simple. Hence, the leader in the church that somehow boasts of his position or uses that position to exert himself over others has joined the ranks of the worldly whom Jesus strongly condemns.

Third, we see that true greatness of leadership is determined not by how many are "under" our leadership, but by how many we *serve* as leaders. The serving in Matthew 20 was of the most demeaning variety: the washing of feet, a gesture of hospitality normally performed by a household slave. Too often, we leaders stay very busy doing good things, but we often limit ourselves to what is easiest for us, rather than what calls us out of our comfort zones. Further, we may find it far more convenient to serve certain types of people than others. Jesus was clearly most attracted to the needs of the downtrodden in society; we, however, may be attracted to persons at the other end of the scale. Let's all evaluate ourselves on this important point, for a worldly view and use of leadership is not restricted to those early disciples.

How Do You Spell Success?

We Americans seem to be obsessed with success to the point that it has been exalted almost to the status of godhood, something to be achieved at nearly any cost. Why are we so driven to achieve? In many cases, I am convinced that our insecurities about ourselves are the root cause.[1] We try to prove ourselves through performance so that others will be impressed with us, thinking we will then feel better about King Self. This issue is not easy to understand because we do have purer motives that are interspersed with the worldly ambitions. But we need to be aware of some of the warning signs of worldly ambition. Although the following list is not intended to be exhaustive, it will get you started in examining your own motives:

[1]See chapter 9, "Escaping the Performance Trap," in my book *The Power of Spiritual Thinking* (Billerica, Mass.: Discipleship Publications International, 2000) 77-84.

- a heightened fear of failure
- an intense spirit of competition
- an emotional dip when you lose even a friendly competition
- a compelling desire to be the best at something, not simply good at it
- a strong need for public recognition
- envy or jealousy toward others who are lifted up when you are not

Make your own list and get in touch with why do you do what you do.

How do you determine success in ministry? For the most part, numerical growth has been our main gauge of success. In fact, we may be afraid to say that our group is growing spiritually and should therefore soon begin growing more numerically—that would be seen as a *cop-out* to some. But as one ministry friend of mine stated, "When growth becomes god, God is God no longer."

Let me venture out a bit farther on the thin ice of self-examination. God expects the church to grow and gave us the Great Commission to help us keep our focus on this expected growth. One of the most firmly established traditions in our movement concerns our use of statistics and numbers. From the outset, let me say that accountability and evaluation are an essential part of any healthy organization. The deeper issue is how we use the numbers in measuring success and how we use them to motivate God's children. The right types of goals certainly have their place, and statistics can be used to measure much more than numerical growth. With care, we can collect data that help us understand where people are in terms of personal prayer and Bible study, building and enriching our families, serving others, and a myriad of other spiritual activities. The problem is that we often measure only activities that directly relate to numerical growth and then end up focusing only on what we thus measure.

For a number of years, I have been concerned about how we motivate the church to be committed and to evangelize. If we use the wrong type of motivation, it begins to work like a drug, in that it takes a bigger and bigger "hit" to get the same result. Eventually, you cannot get the same result no matter how hard you push. I have been convinced for years that we would reach this point in motivating people if we did not become more Biblical in our motivation.

In writing my book *Revolution!*[2] an exposition of Acts, I was struck by the content of the early preachers' messages. Almost exclusively, the emphasis was on Deity—God, Jesus and the Holy Spirit. This led me to think about the emphases in Paul's writings. About half of each of his letters was also on the theme of Deity, and the other half was about loving each other in God's family. Little was ever said directly about the need to evangelize, and little was said about specific growth numbers.

The only baptism numbers mentioned in the whole New Testament are in Acts 2:41 ("about three thousand") and Acts 4:4 ("about five thousand" men). In their day-to-day ministry activities, they may have discussed numbers, but God did not include such in the New Testament. Did the apparent lack of emphasis on calling people to evangelize mean that the Great Commission was not important to the early church or that they had little success in growing the church? Hardly. What becomes apparent is that evangelism was much more a by-product of their emphasis on God and love than a direct focus.

Out of the Overflow

I do not have many conversations in which I do not talk about my wife, my children and their mates (our children through marriage), and our grandchildren. No one tells me to share about them; I share out of the overflow of my heart. The early Christians seemed to have this same response in their relationship to God. In Peter's words, "For we cannot help speaking

[2]Gordon Ferguson, *Revolution! The World-Changing Church in the Book of Acts* (Billerica, Mass.: Discipleship Publications International, 1998).

about what we have seen and heard" (Acts 4:20). What had they seen and heard? In a word, Jesus. He was the focus of their lives and message. They were certainly not gurus of a grow-and-succeed philosophy, and yet they grew. The reason for their growth was their Jesus focus.

Martin Luther had a flaw in his theology about the covenants (Old and New Testaments), in my opinion, but he understood one truth that we vitally need to recognize. When Luther talked of Law and Gospel, he was not distinguishing between the Old Testament and the New Testament as most do when using these terms. Rather, he distinguished between promise (Gospel) and command (Law), between what God has done for us (Gospel) and what we must do in response (Law). He saw Law as only demand and Gospel as only grace. Although he went too far in his approach, he was right in seeing that a focus on God motivates while a focus on man's obedience ultimately demotivates.

If our love for and awe of God are not continually being enlarged, we will run out of spiritual steam somewhere along the way. Most of the pressures faced by the early church were induced by the world; many of ours are self-induced. When Paul mentioned the daily pressure of his concern for all the churches (2 Corinthians 11:28), the pressure came from the needs of the people under his leadership rather than from ministry expectations from other leaders. Obviously, as disciples, we will feel a responsibility and burden for the lost that we didn't feel before. However, coming to Christ should decrease our burdens in so many other areas (Matthew 11:28-30), not increase them. A burdened view of Christianity can certainly be developed through our individual erroneous attitudes, but it can also be developed by allowing Christ's religion to become an organization rather than an organism, a system rather than a spiritual family.

The Three Ms

Most religious groups through the ages have followed the man/movement/monument path. Briefly stated, this means God raises up a man whose message stirs the hearts of others. A movement is begun that grows and thrives. Eventually, however, the fire is lost and instead of going on to greater heights, men build a monument to what has happened. They live off past glories and put out the Spirit's desire to move things forward. Judaism, in spite of the repeated warnings of the prophets, became an ineffective system. Early Christianity, in spite of its original vibrancy and growth, became an ineffective system. Our present movement has, in some ways, certainly in some places, already started showing signs of following this pattern. Of course, we can readily point to many good signs, praise God, but we must be willing to do the self-examination that allows us to make corrections before our unproductive or even un-Biblical habits become entrenched. I love the movement we are part of and will always thank God for it. This makes me want to allow God to continually show us what needs to change—instead of defensively trying to maintain the status quo.

To make my point perfectly clear, we need to return to a much greater focus on God, with much less of a focus on worldly views of success. I am thankful that the Boston church is the largest congregation of any type in New England, but this is not the issue. The issue is how closely we adhere to the word of God and imitate his Son, in whom all the treasures of wisdom and knowledge are hidden (Colossians 2:3). I am not into competing with the religious world, both because the playing field is not level—they can lure attendees in all sorts of worldly ways—and because that is not the directive of God. I am into being as much like Jesus as possible and finding out from the Bible how he defines success. On that note, read through Matthew 25:31-46 to see how successful your ministry is according to this standard of measurement. Here, Jesus speaks about feeding the hungry, lodging the stranger, clothing the unclothed and visiting the sick and imprisoned. He does not talk about evangelizing, by the way, but anyone who loves people enough to serve in all these ways could not help but share the only truly good news with those being served.

I am not trying to be unnecessarily critical, but I am trying hard to say that we have more of a system than we imagine, and like all systems, we exalt certain things and omit others—which may or may not be approved by God. Religious organizations tend to pattern themselves after what they admire most in society. Not surprisingly, the second and third century church began to pattern itself organizationally after the Roman government. What do we admire in our modern day society? The answer is probably corporate America, especially in its organization and definition of success. But we must be careful. Numerical growth is one of the things that brings glory to God, as Paul said in 2 Corinthians 4:15: "All this is for your benefit, so that the grace that is reaching more and more people may cause thanksgiving to overflow to the glory of God." However, it is not the only thing. Jesus gave us the Great Commission, but the purpose of the church is not to grow; the purpose is to glorify God in time and in eternity. Certainly, an essential part of that purpose on earth is the mission of sharing Jesus with the world. If the overall, deeper purpose of glorifying God is really our focus, we will grow—but growth is not our eternal purpose. It is our earthly mission. Thus, it is perilous for us to take as our models those organizations that are just concerned with the bottom line.

A New View of Sundays

Since we are talking about purpose here, let's get more specific about another current practice of ours. What was the primary purpose of Sunday meetings for the early church? What I see in the New Testament is that these meetings of the body were designed primarily to be, well, *meetings of the body*. They were not expressly evangelistic. Certainly, an unbeliever would be welcomed, and 1 Corinthians 14:24 mentions that possibility in terms of "if an unbeliever...comes in." Our meetings are attractive to outsiders, and even when we are preaching directly to the body, visitors are impressed with our focus on the Bible and honesty about our sins. But the New Testament does not portray first-day-of-the-week meetings primarily as evangelistic. These meetings were apparently designed to provide an uninterrupted opportunity to worship God as a group, thereby recharging their spiritual batteries to face the world and be evangelistic in the upcoming week.

When we as the modern-day church relied on Bible discussion groups in our homes, apartments and dorm rooms for our primary evangelistic outreach, we were closer to what we find in the practices of the first century church. I am glad that we seem to be moving back in this direction. Properly functioning Bible discussion groups actually accomplish a number of good ends, including providing disciples with a family setting in the home, the opportunity for them to share in a group and thereby raise up as leaders, and of course, an effective way of reaching the lost. Without such settings, more dependence on paid ministry staff develops, which is tied into the clergy/laity feeling that we seem to have in many places.

Is having an evangelistic thrust on Sundays wrong? I would not go that far, to be sure, but I am increasingly concerned that we not make significant changes in what the early church did without really studying out the purposes behind their practices. Many of the Sunday sermons I hear are almost exclusively directed at non-Christians, and many of the midweek meetings I have attended are occasions when three things are emphasized: give your money; hear the announcements; get more visitors for Sunday. When do we hear those meaty, uplifting messages that draw us to God and change our hearts? How are we going to develop the heart that characterized the first century church and led them to evangelize their world? We need change, radical change, if we are going to restore that original Christianity.

Refocusing

We must emphasize what the Bible emphasizes. As Paul described in Colossians 1:28, "We proclaim him, admonishing and teaching everyone with all wisdom, so that we may present everyone perfect in Christ." This is the purpose to which we must return. I do not propose to have all the answers about how to accomplish this, but we must begin making changes where changes are obviously needed and then trust God to direct our steps from there. Whatever keeps our focus on God will prove to be the correct course. Let's have the conviction and courage to do it—to his glory!

3

The Power Behind Leadership
F

I recently had a conversation with Tom Jones, who has been the principal editor for the books I have published. As God would have it, he shared some thoughts with me that were destined to find their way into this book. Tom is characterized by a humility and spiritual discernment that few can equal, and his Biblical insights deserve a broader reading. The observations he shared from a lesson he had just delivered to several ministry groups affected me greatly. Thus, much of what is in this chapter comes from his lesson.

Of Primary Importance

What do you think is the power behind leadership? We all say "God's power," but is that what we really believe and rely on? Probably not. We rely on ourselves far more than we think. Almost from birth, we begin building the kingdom of Self, and nothing short of the Son of God's death on the cross can ever break our self-promoting ways. No wonder a requisite of following Jesus is denying self (Mark 8:34, Luke 9:23). Our most pervasive sins are pride and selfishness, and they are the root from which almost all other sins spring. If we were somehow divinely enabled to see the full magnitude of these sins all at once, we might not be able to survive the emotional shock. God is merciful, however, and he only leads us to see our unsavory qualities a bit at a time. But we must see more and change more deeply as leaders if we are to lead others to the cross. Prayerfully, the thoughts in this chapter can prompt such change.

No leadership topic is more important than this one, and if we do not understand it, other topics will ultimately not matter anyway. If we fail to grasp God's plan to give us strength, we will (1) wear out trying to lead or (2) fail to produce godly results even if we stay in the fight. The result will be the squandering of leadership opportunities. Continually attempting to do even godly things in our own strength will lead to the same spiritual calamities that the Israelites of old faced.

> "I will break down your stubborn pride and make the sky above you like iron and the ground beneath you like bronze. Your strength will be spent in vain, because your soil will not yield its crops, nor will the trees of the land yield their fruit." (Leviticus 26:19-20)

On the other hand, if we do understand where to get strength, no challenge of leadership will be too great. Nothing will wear us down or cause us to quit. We may struggle and we may hurt—but we will not quit, and we most certainly will see amazing things happen.

We must understand this principle: Seeing great things happen in the church is not determined by the talent of the group. It is determined by our understanding of and our convictions about how to gain strength for the task. But let me issue a warning. Understanding and having life-changing convictions about God's will in this area requires great humility and a great change of mind, even for many of us who have been disciples and leaders for a long time.

Leading from Weakness

The biggest mistake we make as leaders is when we take stock of our strengths and weaknesses, and then we rely on our strengths. What are some natural strengths that others have told you that you have—or that you have figured out that you have?

1. intellectual ability
2. logical mind

3. organizational skills
4. oratory skills (public speaking)
5. sense of humor
6. determination
7. willingness to work hard
8. persuasive personality
9. perseverance

Often when we are not doing well, our first thought is, *I need to snap out of this.* We foolishly think we can go back and rely on our strengths to get where we need to be spiritually. Wrong, wrong, wrong! While different ones among us have strengths that God can use, here is the ultimate truth: If we try to lead spiritually by relying on our strengths, we are doomed to fail.

Relying on our strengths leads to arrogance, pride, competitiveness and humanism. Of course, all of these lead to spiritual defeat. "God opposes the proud but gives grace to the humble" (1 Peter 5:5). The Old Testament prophets addressed the problem head-on:

> Woe to those who go down to Egypt for help,
>> who rely on horses,
> who trust in the multitude of their chariots
>> and in the great strength of their horsemen,
> but do not look to the Holy One of Israel,
>> or seek help from the LORD. (Isaiah 31:1)

> This is what the LORD says:

> "Cursed is the one who trusts in man,
>> who depends on flesh for his strength
>> and whose heart turns away from the LORD."
> (Jeremiah 17:5)

> But you have planted wickedness,
>> you have reaped evil,
>> you have eaten the fruit of deception.
> Because you have depended on your own strength
>> and on your many warriors.... (Hosea 10:13)

Spiritual leadership is not the art of taking all that is learned in the corporate world or the political world (God forbid) or the world of education or the world of the street and applying it to leading in the church. But sometimes we think it is, and perhaps by default, we often act like it is. Spiritual leadership first and foremost involves *being spiritual*. And being spiritual first and foremost involves crucifying our dependence on self and replacing it with reliance on God.

Trying to provide spiritual leadership in a worldly way has a long history. Peter was one of the chief transgressors. He left everything to follow Jesus. He signed on to be a messianic crusader. But when he heard Jesus talk about suffering and dying in weakness on a cross, he took Jesus aside (nice of him!) and corrected him. "'Never, Lord!' he said. 'This shall never happen to you!'" (Matthew 16:22). Peter was relying on his great intellectual gifts, his vast knowledge of Scripture, his logical mind and primarily his understanding of how things worked *in the streets*. But listen to what Jesus said to him:

> Jesus turned and said to Peter, "Get behind me, Satan! You are a stumbling block to me; you do not have in mind the things of God, but the things of men." (Matthew 16:23)

Peter's problem was the problem we often have. We try to lead in the kingdom, but we have in mind the things of men rather than the things of God. We say spiritual things, and we pray spiritual-sounding prayers, but underneath it all, we rely on our flesh. No wonder Jesus later said to Peter:

> "Simon, Simon, Satan has asked to sift you as wheat. But I have prayed for you, Simon, that your faith may not fail. And when you have turned back, strengthen your brothers." (Luke 22:31-32)

The King James Version translates *epistrepho* in Greek ("turned back" in the NIV) as "when you are converted"—when you have changed, when you have turned from the wrong way to the right way. Peter could help others find strength only when he learned to find it not in himself or in man's wisdom, but only in God. Consider these passages:

> "The LORD is my strength and my song;
>   he has become my salvation.
> He is my God, and I will praise him,
>   my father's God, and I will exalt him." (Exodus 15:2)

> My flesh and my heart may fail,
>   but God is the strength of my heart
>   and my portion forever. (Psalm 73:26)

> But those who hope in the LORD
>   will renew their strength.
> They will soar on wings like eagles;
>   they will run and not grow weary,
>   they will walk and not be faint. (Isaiah 40:31)

Becoming God-Reliant

We truly rely on God by focusing on our weaknesses and on God's call to lead his people. It is an awesome call—one far too heavy to carry out on our own. As a result, the principle expressed in Matthew 5:3 will be fulfilled:

> "Blessed are the poor in spirit,
>   for theirs is the kingdom of heaven."

We will say, "Woe is me. I need help," like in Isaiah 6. We will say, "I have this awesome responsibility, but I can't handle it. My flesh and my heart fail me." At first this does not feel good, but it *is* good! This will lead us to rely on God.

Isn't this what Paul told the Corinthians that God was teaching him?

> But this happened that we might not rely on ourselves but on God, who raises the dead. (2 Corinthians 1:9)

> To keep me from becoming conceited because of these surpassingly great revelations, there was given me a thorn in my flesh, a messenger of Satan, to torment me. Three times I pleaded with the Lord to take it away from me. But he said to me, "My grace is sufficient for you, for my power is made perfect in weakness." Therefore I will boast all the more gladly about my weaknesses, so that Christ's power may rest on me. (2 Corinthians 12:7-9)

God will allow different circumstances to take away our self-reliance, and we must learn to be grateful for all of these. Confidence in the flesh must be stripped away by every means God may choose to use. We must lead with his strength and not our own.

I told you this would require a mind change. This is the exact opposite of what we hear from the self-esteem, self-help movement, and the exact opposite of what you would be told in success seminars. We first of all need to get fully in touch with how weak we are. But then we must do what Paul did—we must express faith. Even as we confess that we are weak, we express confidence that Christ's power will rest on us. We must learn to say with Paul:

> Such confidence as this is ours through Christ before God. Not that we are competent in ourselves to claim anything for ourselves, but our competence comes from God. (2 Corinthians 3:4-5)

Notice the balance: We are not proud and self-confident, but we are confident in God. We have the strength to lead, but not the pride that will defeat us. We must say, as Paul did in Philippians 4:13, "I can do everything through him who gives me strength." The strength to lead is a gift from God—a gift he freely gives to those who ask with the right motives (James 4:3).

But What About My Gifts?

One of the tensions you may feel in reading these thoughts is in squaring the concept of boasting in your weaknesses with exercising the God-given gifts that Romans 12 talks about. Obviously, these gifts are strengths to be used for God and his kingdom. In the context of Romans 12, Paul mentions at least two vital keys to understanding and using our gifts before he actually mentions the gifts themselves. He warns against conforming to the pattern of the world (v2), and certainly one of the most established patterns of this world is to trust in self instead of God. Then he writes:

> For by the grace given me I say to every one of you: Do not think of yourself more highly than you ought, but rather think of yourself with sober judgment, in accordance with the measure of faith God has given you. (Romans 12:3)

At this point, those of us influenced by the self-esteem gurus are quick to exclaim, "But we shouldn't think of ourselves more lowly than we ought either." I do not disagree with this observation, but God did not seem to think it necessary to "balance out" what he inspired Paul to write. When you stop to think about it, the Bible simply does not focus on the need for us humans to raise our low self-images. Even the passages we use for this purpose are few and mostly taken out of context. For example, we may quote Matthew 22:39, "Love your neighbor as yourself," and then say, "See, it says we should love ourselves." Do you really think that this was Jesus' point here? Or we look at Philippians 2:4, which says, "Each of you should look not only to your own interests, but also to the interests of others." And we say, "See, it says that we should look to our own interests." In this passage the New International Version translation appears to be more based on our culture than on the Greek of the passage. The New Revised Standard Version is quite literal in showing the hyperbole (overstatement to make a point): "Let each of you look *not* to your own interests, but to the interests of others" (emphasis added). Read the context of the verse and you will see that the self-image activists are grabbing at straws.

What does the Bible say about building a great self-image? Nothing, directly. The focus is never on man, but on God. The more you see God, the more you see your own sin ("Go away from me, Lord; I am a sinful man!"—Luke 5:8) and the more you will be amazed that you are somehow still so important and special to God. Focus on self and you will be weak and miserable; focus on God and you will be unexpectedly exalted, for in spite of our sinfulness, he stoops down to make us great (Psalm 18:35).

My value is not based on my performance, nor is yours. At our best, our performance is quite flawed. As newborns, my young grandchildren did not offer much in the way of performance. They did little else besides cry and make messes in their diapers! Yet, we all huddled around them as if they were the center of the universe. Why? Little bundles of humanity made in the image of the Creator had entered our midst, and this is nothing short of miraculous. Our value is determined by the nature we get from the Father of our spirits (Hebrews 12:9) and by the death of God in the flesh for each of us. Woe to those whose self-images are based on anything else, and woe to the leader who thinks his or her power really comes through talent, intellect and achievement.

Our competence and confidence must come from God. Though we may be steeped in the deadly doctrines of humanism, the advance of God's plan for planet Earth depends on our escape from their grasp. He may allow us to start on the leadership path with misguided ideas, but he will only allow us to stay on it for a lifetime if we learn this lesson. As Peter put it, "Humble yourselves, therefore, under God's mighty hand, that he may lift you up in due time" (1 Peter 5:6). Just when is the due time? When we are so focused on God that we no longer want any credit for what he has accomplished through us. Let's humble out and let him use us in ways that will stagger our imaginations, while bringing him all the glory!

4

Building Team in the Church Family

F

One of leadership's most fundamental tasks is to build team spirit in the church family. Some physical families work fairly well as a team, but are lacking in deep relationships. Others feel deeply about one another, but do not work well together in accomplishing family goals. The key is in blending the two, with close working relationships that move everyone joyfully toward desired goals.

As leaders, we may or may not be doing this well. If you are on the ministry staff, you would do well to ask the leaders whom you lead, staff and nonstaff, to evaluate you in terms of how you build team and family. What I have consistently found is that some leaders are not in touch with reality—they *think* that they understand and apply these leadership principles much better than they actually *do*. Without evaluation beyond ourselves, we will not get the big picture. So read carefully, but determine to enlist others to evaluate your leadership and the condition of the group you lead. It will prove very worthwhile.

In this chapter, we will examine important basic principles for building team in the family of God.

Building Team Through Discipling

Most of us know the power of a group to disciple its members effectively—often better than any one person could disciple any other person—since the group has a broader perspective than any one of its members. More eyes see more things. Additionally, the group has a greater impact in giving perspective, by sheer virtue of numbers. When one person points out something, his or her words can be more easily dismissed as mere opinion; when five people say the same thing, we are more apt to own up to what is being said.

Just who is the "team" who does the discipling? We most often think about a more mature Christian discipling a less mature one, which is quite natural. Jesus did it this way with his disciples, so it has to be good! Practically, in so many settings, peers disciple peers, which is also very effective. We have been trained to be submissive to those "over" us in the Lord, but when peers disciple us, different "buttons" are pushed, exposing the heart even better. However, at times, an even broader perspective is good, in which those "under" us are able to give their perspective into our lives. For those who are leaders, providing for this kind of input does much to eliminate an "us and them" mentality. It also reveals some things about us that we might never see otherwise.

A few years ago, Theresa and I were working with a couple on staff who had begun to have some challenges with their teen and preteen children. We gave them input that we knew had to be pretty accurate, pointing out some marriage and parenting dynamics that had contributed to the family challenges. The couple was slow to come around to what we said, so we encouraged them to receive input from other couples who knew them well. One of these couples was on staff with them, and one was a mature family group leader couple. Thus, each couple knew those being discipled from a somewhat different perspective. The impact was truly amazing, with the nonstaff couple having the most impact in some ways because of their grass-roots perspective.

Leaders, especially those on staff, must ask for more input than they typically do from those whom they lead. The forum may vary, but the need is absolute. Moms and dads do well to ask their children for input, and the spiritual application is that the "children" under our charge need the opportunity to give us helpful input. It helps both them and us. Most of us welcome the opportunity to give our perspective to those who lead us.

Golden Rule leadership in this case means we ask others to give us what we would want our leaders to ask of us.

Building Team Through Making Key Decisions

No one person has the perspective and judgment that a group does, period. My trust for a group to talk through and make decisions has been developed over a period of many years with all kinds of groups. Most organizations not only recognize this dynamic, but also recognize that the perspectives must vary if the group is to be effective. However, an insecure leader will seek leaders under him who are essentially yes-men, and he will chafe if they question his opinions. This leadership style is not only ineffective, it is dangerous because it lacks the checks and balances that any healthy group must have.

Jim McCartney is one of our key church administrators in Boston and came to us with a wealth of practical experience from the corporate world. One of his many responsibilities is to serve as a business consultant to Discipleship Publications International. Almost three years ago, he led the managers and advisors of DPI through several days of planning and decision-making in what he called a "strategic planning session." (This has now become an annual event.) He combined his training in the business world with spiritual principles as he chaired the meetings. One of his key principles during our lengthy brainstorming phases was that everyone in the group was equal. This proved to be a vital principle, for everyone felt their voice was important and was going to be heard. Similarly, leaders who do not short-circuit the input stage before moving to the decision-making stage utilize the great power of a group.

Because the need for those with different perspectives is so vital, United States law now requires nonprofit organizations to include nonemployees on their boards of directors. This is the case with the Board of Directors for the Boston Church of Christ, and the variations among us lead to broadened viewpoints that we would not otherwise have. (By the way, this book was edited by four different editors with four different perspectives. I can tell this as I see all the changes in different colors on my word processor. But each perspective is valuable.) Overall, my conviction is that we leaders in the church do not involve the grassroots members enough in the decision-making process.

Read the following passages to see how the early church was involved in a major decision at what we now call the Jerusalem Conference.

> The apostles and elders met to consider this question. (Acts 15:6)

> Then the apostles and elders, with the whole church, decided to choose some of their own men and send them to Antioch with Paul and Barnabas. They chose Judas (called Barsabbas) and Silas, two men who were leaders among the brothers. (Acts 15:22)

The sequence here is very important. The leaders from Antioch, after "sharp dispute and debate" over Gentile issues (Acts 15:2), were sent to meet with the leaders of the Jerusalem church, namely the apostles and elders. It was in this setting that the issues were discussed and decisions reached. Then, the whole church was brought in and informed of the discussions and the decisions, and their involvement was sought in deciding how to disseminate the decisions. The church is not a democracy, and the leaders are responsible for deciding the weightier issues and maintaining sound doctrine (1 Timothy 1:3, Titus 1:9)—make no mistake about that. However, the church must be involved in the decision-making process at appropriate levels if it is to be a family. In Acts 15 we see that the disciples were brought in and informed in a way that they appreciated, and they were involved in deciding how and by whom the decisions would be spread.

Previously, as seen in Acts 6, another decision was made in a similar manner regarding how to meet the needs of neglected widows. The apostles decided how the problem would be solved, and then they asked the congregation to select the men to carry out their plan.

The balance between the leadership making key decisions and involving the church in the institution of those decisions is a *huge* issue. When leaders do not make decisions and lead, either chaos or inertia results. But when those being led do not sense that their opinions are valued, equally damaging results ensue. One well-educated, mature brother with a very successful career once made this comment to me: "On my job, my ideas are not only welcomed, but I may be paid extra for them if they are good. In the church, the leaders don't seem to want to know what I think." Judges 5:2 describes the happy occasion when leadership and "followership" work well together: "When the princes in Israel take the lead, when the people willingly offer themselves—praise the LORD!" Respect of followers for leaders and leaders for followers must be present in our hearts, expressed in our words and put into action as we labor together. We are all part of the one body described in 1 Corinthians 12, in which no one is superior and no one is inferior. Different roles we do have, but different value as children of God, we do not have. We are a family and we are a team. As such, we must learn to make and implement decisions together.

Building Team Through Planning

Truthfully, only a few of us leaders are creative enough and detail-oriented enough to plan everything—or almost everything—on our own. I think our world sector leader, Randy McKean, comes as close to being able to do so as just about anyone I know. But as good as he is, his commitment to the team concept has become greater and greater with the increase in size and age of our world sector. Most of us are not nearly as good, which means that we all must learn how to build and utilize team leadership.

Six years ago, I was asked to spearhead the development of a curriculum for the kingdom children's ministry. Even though

I have a degree in music education, my teaching experience was never with young children; nor have I, because of other responsibilities, ever taught in the children's ministry in the church. The task looked formidable in the early stages and absolutely overwhelming once we started to see the bigger picture. Was it panic time? Almost, but not quite.

Like American auto executive Lee Iococca once said of himself, my creative leadership ability consists mainly in knowing how to surround myself with creative leaders. I sought out the best help available and formed an advisory committee consisting primarily of the children's ministry staffs of the churches in Boston and New York City. Even with this group, our ignorance about developing such a broad-based curriculum was exceeded only by our determination to get the job done. With the help of DPI, and especially of Larry Wood and Sheila Jones, we were later all amazed at what God did in just five years. From beginning to end, I knew (and still know) less about children's ministry than any other person on the committee, including my wife, who has both the education and teaching experience with children. One thing I do know: Choose the right group, lead it well, and the sky's the limit.

Leaders who feel that they must do the bulk of the planning themselves in order to be good leaders are naive, arrogant or unwise. Group leadership is needed for many aspects of planning—monthly calendars, Sunday and midweek services (a month or more in advance), and special activities of all types. It is hugely important to have those with different mind-sets involved in the planning process. However, let me add one important caution here. Young churches led by young leaders will not find themselves surrounded by a lot of other mature disciples in the early stages, but they must begin raising up others to be a part of the leadership team. Leaders in this position must also seek consistent input from both peers in similar ministry situations and from their disciplers.

Some time ago, an important truth dawned on me. Church leadership can function well only with the cooperation of two different perspectives among us. In Maxwell Maltz's book, *Psycho-cybernetics*,[1] which I read as a young man, the author describes the two ways our computer-like minds process information. In one scenario, we may know the results we are after, and as we focus on them, our minds figure out and fill in the process by which they can be achieved. On the other hand, we may know many of the components involved in a project, but not the ultimate results, and as we focus on these pieces of the big picture, our minds themselves produce the specific answers. In the former approach, we know the answer and must discover the steps to achieve that answer; in the latter approach, we know some of the steps, but not the ultimate answer. Essentially, Maltz' theory reminds me of the evangelist/elder approach to processing an issue.

The evangelist focuses mainly on one bottom-line issue: numerical growth of his ministry—which is his job. The elder, by definition, is an "overseer." He looks over the health of the whole church in a broader way, which includes motivation, contentment and the number of people leaving the church, as well as the reasons for all these. He is concerned with the growth of the church, but he feels less responsibility and pressure for short-term growth, which allows him to think about the underlying long-term principles that ultimately influence the growth rate. Obviously, the evangelist is also concerned with long-term principles and the elder is also concerned with short-term, numerical growth—but the perspectives are somewhat different by design. Sadly, those in each role may not appreciate their need for the other's viewpoint enough. Worse, they may not trust the other's perspective and can even grow to resent it. However, both perspectives are necessary to the *team*, and we must understand the natural tendencies and necessities of each.

[1]Maxwell Maltz, *Psycho-cybernetics* (Englewood Cliffs, N.J.: Prentice-Hall, 1960).

Practically speaking, one very obvious challenge in the elder/evangelist dynamic is the limited number of elders available to work with evangelists. Most churches do not even have elders and likely will not for some time, which means that even young evangelists must do two things: (1) learn to think both long- and short-term quickly and (2) train qualified people to function as shepherds until elders are available. Younger and smaller churches can meet both needs adequately if the leader understands and accepts the challenge presented. One potential solution in some situations might be to reconsider our practice of insisting on a plurality of elders before any one can be appointed. The kingdom teachers have had Biblical discussions regarding our view on the subject—a dialogue prompted by Marty Wooten. All of us see a plurality as the Biblical example and certainly as the ideal, but none of us would bind our current practice. We agree that the appointment of one elder is possible as an interim approach to establishing a full-fledged eldership.

Another helpful approach is to identify those leaders who tend to have elder-type mind-sets (often the older ministry staff brothers) to work closely with the evangelists. Interestingly, after delivering a lesson on this topic in a Boston church staff meeting, it was pointed out to me that an evangelist's wife may have more of what I have called the "elder's perspective" and thus be able to contribute this perspective to her husband's thinking. It does seem to me that our wives may be more attuned to how ministry decisions affect the average disciple. The current emphasis on Spiritual Recovery in many of our churches addresses this need directly and should help tremendously.[2] Bottom line, the different perspectives of elders and evangelists must not be seen as conflicting and potentially adversarial, but as absolutely essential in dealing with both the big picture and with short-term growth.

---

[2] This refers to special efforts led by mature and experienced leaders, focused on those who are weaker. The goal is to help struggling disciples, or those who may be in danger of leaving, to feel heard and understood and to be put in a family environment where their faith can be renewed.

I wish that all elders would have the type of relationship with their lead evangelist that Wyndham and I have with Randy. We are learning to work well as a team. It is my opinion that in the kingdom we have given far too little consideration to long-range principles and are reaping serious consequences in both growth and in the number of people who leave. We must not panic or be prophets of doom, but we must look more deeply at the long-term building principles—of which building family is one of the most important. In chapter 7, Wyndham will look at the elder/evangelist relationship in much more detail.

Building Team Through Esprit de Corps

Feeling a part of the successes of a group is vital to building a spirit of team. The concept of producing "group fruit" needs to be emphasized. When the whole group is encouraged to be involved in someone becoming a disciple and everyone is made to feel that they contribute, this goes a long way toward building family, not to mention having a positive impact evangelistically. Feeling appreciated is perhaps the most important ingredient in building a spirit of team—and one of the most overlooked. Because of our focus on the short-term aspect of the mission (numerical growth during a given goal period), we tend to hold up those whose immediate evangelistic efforts and effects are easily seen and measured. However, others who steadfastly maintain the disciple's lifestyle and are developing spiritual character are often overlooked. Ultimately, the impact of our lives will be measured on a long-term basis. As the disciple-making chain runs its course, only God will know the full extent of the impact our lives are going to make.

Who Is Important?

In my book *Revolution! The World-Changing Church in the Book of Acts*, I made some observations about a widow named Tabitha or Dorcas (see Acts 9:36) that will serve us well here.[3] Dorcas was an older woman who was known for her work as a

[3]Gordon Ferguson, *Revolution! The World-Changing Church in the Book of Acts* (Billerica, Mass.: Discipleship Publications International, 1998) 98.

seamstress, for doing good and helping the poor. Why is her story in the Bible, and why did Peter focus his attention on her? She was not a high-profile leader and certainly not a big financial contributor. From man's perspective, she was not all that impressive, but she appeared to have impressed God and her circle of widow friends. Jesus often talked of widows and held a number of them up as great spiritual examples. His brother James had this to say:

> Religion that God our Father accepts as pure and faultless is this: to look after orphans and widows in their distress and to keep oneself from being polluted by the world. (James 1:27)

How do you think widows feel in our fellowship: appreciated and useful, or fairly unimportant? Why don't you ask them? The answer may prove to be revealing.

We often praise the same people or types of people over and over. They are the ones who are effective at the things we treasure most, the things that are most directly connected with numerical growth. Obviously, we are in a revolution and the importance of the mission to evangelize is paramount. But we still are missing something. The problem is that we do not understand the church as a "body" well enough. This has to do with the most commonly used word describing the church in the New Testament. We are not just a body of people when we gather to worship together; we are the body of Christ, responsible for revealing him to the world. Paul said that corporately we are the fullness of Christ, and when people behold the church functioning as it should, they see Christ in action—but no one of us is his fullness.

Every member is important, even though we do not all have the same gifts (maybe *especially* because we do not all have the same gifts). Study through Romans 12 and 1 Corinthians 12. In my book *Romans: The Heart Set Free*,[4] in discussing Romans 12, I looked at how our terminology about ministry

[4] Gordon Ferguson, *Romans: The Heart Set Free* (Billerica, Mass.: Discipleship Publications International, 2001).

staff positions can make nonstaff people feel. I highly recommend that you read those comments. One key point there is that all disciples have a ministry (2 Corinthians 5:18), and all disciples are to be full-time (living) sacrifices (Romans 12:1). Therefore, all disciples are in the full-time ministry in a real sense of the word! The accurate distinction is that some are church-supported and others are self-supported—but we are all full-time ministry people in a definite sense. I believe that this distinction is not simply a trivial matter of terminology, but that it affects the way we see ourselves and therefore, affects our effectiveness for the Lord.

Paul states in 1 Corinthians 12:22 that "those parts of the body that seem to be weaker are indispensable." Is that really how we feel about weaker members or older members or sicker members? Now that I am old enough to qualify for senior discounts in at least a few places, I would like to know! What I think is that we have a lot to learn about the value of different kinds of people with different types of gifts, and how they all contribute to the effectiveness of our mission.

What Is Important?

Do we value the little things that people do for God and for others in his name, or do we only see the more obvious kinds of impact that are being made? It's a good question, isn't it? Sometimes it appears to me that we are afraid to hold up people for the little things, as if that will lower the emphasis on evangelism. Everything that falls under the definition of "good" is important and, done properly, has some place in carrying out our overriding mission of reaching the world with the message of Christ. He who gave the Great Commission—and died for it—had this to say about the matter: "I tell you the truth, anyone who gives you a cup of water in my name because you belong to Christ will certainly not lose his reward" (Mark 9:41).

In the church we have many unsung heroes who serve in a multitude of different ways behind the scenes. We have *too* many of them—not because they should not serve in these ways, but because they should not remain unnoticed and unsung. God can open hearts in quite ordinary ways. Once my wife called a woman to try to study the Bible with her, but she happened to be ill that day and was not too interested in studying anyway. Theresa made a chicken pie (yes, from scratch!) and drove a long distance in a snowstorm to deliver it. To this day, the woman, who is now right with God, attributes her heart change to that act of kindness. It is the word of God that brings people to faith, but the Word must be read in the lives of people just as surely as in the "Good Book."[4]

Every disciple is special, and all of us are going to have to learn to make each other *feel* special. Those of us who are parents have hopefully figured out the absolute necessity of building up our children and helping them to have self-worth and a high self-esteem. And we have learned that our less talented youngsters need it the most. Now we must learn the same lessons in dealing with God's kids—all of them—especially the weaker ones. Peter had been with Jesus too long not to have time for the "little people." And because he had this heart, God used these kindnesses to get Peter in just the right place at the right time to use those "kingdom keys" once more.

I pray that this chapter first of all promotes healthy thinking, discussion and self-examination. Then, with wisdom, it can be applied in appropriate ways to your ministry situation. Building the kingdom by building family in the church is more important than most of us realize. Building the kingdom by building team is just as important. When we combine these two fundamental elements, we and those whom we lead will be blessed immeasurably—and the kingdom will experience the spiritual and numerical growth that God wants it to have!

5

Leadership Style
Team Leadership

F

Leadership style is one of the most important issues in a book about leadership in the kingdom of God. Frankly, if we find ourselves primarily following an ineffective model, we will only end up frustrated and unsuccessful. As you read this chapter, keep your mind and heart open and your defenses down. You will likely find that you lead via some concepts that are taken to task (in love). But if you are a disciple, a true learner—you will find your leadership raised to a level that brings greatly increased effectiveness and joy to you and to those whom you lead. Do you want to be a great leader? Good. Then settle in and read carefully.

Decisive Leadership

In describing a leader, it is common to hear something along these lines: "He is a great leader; he is so decisive." It is true that all great leaders are decisive. But what does being a great, decisive leader really mean?

My most recent foray into this subject was prompted by a young man's desire to become a great leader in his relationship with his girlfriend. She had the more dominant, outgoing personality of the two, and by comparison, he seemed to be fairly reserved in personality and demeanor. He was somewhat anxious, as he wondered if he could really be the strong, decisive leader in the relationship.

I asked him what he thought being such a strong leader with her would entail. In essence, he said, "I would need to think through most everything involving our relationship, figure out what was best and then lead her in those directions." No wonder he was anxious! His definition of decisive leadership boiled down to being an expert in all phases of opposite-sex relationships, being able to always determine the best thing to do in any circumstance and making absolute decisions based on his opinions. Wow, what a burden! Yet, many leaders and would-be leaders assume that decisive leadership involves just such an approach.

A scripture that is descriptive of great leadership, but is rarely applied to leadership is Proverbs 18:17:

> The first to present his case seems right,
>   till another comes forward and questions him.

The one-man-show type of leader violates this passage from the very outset by what he thinks leadership is all about. He decides everything himself, and it all seems very right to him in his self-contained system of reasoning.

I read a recent interview of a former CEO for one of the world's largest and richest companies. He talked about leaders who are only comfortable with a high degree of control over the situations they lead. Not surprisingly, he called them control freaks. They think they have the best ideas, and they want those whom they lead to simply value their opinions and decisions as highly as they themselves do—and to then feel privileged to help them carry them out. Interestingly, at least to football fans, he described Bill Parcells as this type of coach and noted that while he was great at one-year turn arounds, he was never able to sustain a great team with his leadership style. These are my sentiments exactly, having observed Parcells for a number of years with a number of teams.

Many leaders understand only one application of Proverbs 18:17, notably the need to hear both sides of a dispute between marriage partners or other disciples who have unresolved relational challenges. Those of us who have done much counseling know that one person's viewpoint in a relationship is rarely one hundred percent correct, and the other side's view must be heard before firm conclusions are reached. Therefore, if we are wise, we do not form a hard-and-fast conclusion until we have heard both sides. But we often totally miss other important applications of the verse, one of which is how we make decisions as leaders.

A truly great leader has the humility to realize that he does not know everything about every subject. Hopefully, he even has the humility to realize that he does not know nearly as much as he *thinks* he does. He knows that he can be wrong and that he assuredly does not know how to consistently choose between good, better and best without the help of others. By now you are hopefully realizing that great leadership is actually team leadership.

Team Leadership

The captain of *Star Trek: The Next Generation* understands team leadership. He often calls together his top leaders to ask them their opinions on important decisions to be made. He listens carefully as they share their insights and follows up by questioning them to make sure he understands exactly what they are saying. After making his decision, even then he allows them to question it. Sometimes he changes his decision as they provide further input and sometimes he does not. But he is the best kind of leader—one who seeks much input and is then decisive.

A controlling leader produces reactions and results in those whom he leads that he neither understands nor appreciates. They do not feel valued or appreciated, for they do not really have a voice in major decisions. He comes to them with decisions already made, and the best that they can hope for is to fine-tune the decisions or to perhaps block some of them—which makes everyone uncomfortable and does little to deepen relationships and brighten the working atmosphere. Additionally, the secondary leaders do not own the decisions to the full extent and therefore do not accept the responsibility when they fail. And the top leader feels that those leaders who question him are not really loyal. He is then drawn to younger leaders who have not yet matured and are still motivated by his controlling style of leadership. Let me hasten to say that one of the most important tasks of a mature leader is raising up young leaders.[1] We just need to make sure that we are doing it to build God's kingdom and not our own.

Many ministry leaders fear that by asking for others' opinions, they will open themselves up to bad attitudes if they do not go in the direction of the feedback they receive. Somehow we assume that asking for input and ideas is what starts people thinking and developing opinions, which may lead to disappointment if their ideas are not implemented. Mark this down: *People are already thinking and are replete with opinions whether you ask for them or not.* Further, having the people you lead express their opinions cannot be construed as negative no matter what the ultimate decisions turn out to be. Just ask yourself how a wife responds if her husband is either too proud or too fearful to ask for her input. How do the older children feel in the same circumstance? Will the family really be better off if opinions are squelched by the family leader? The answer is obvious, isn't it? Then how will God's family be better off with this sort of leadership, which is, after all, not in line with the Golden Rule?

In church leadership, many leaders tend strongly toward the one-man show type of leadership. It is helpful to understand how this model developed if we are to change it. In the campus ministry days (when committed leadership was young in age), the campus minister would go into an existing traditional church to begin his ministry with young people. Since he worked with mostly newer converts, he was much like a parent

[1] For some pertinent remarks about the need for more, and more zealous, young leaders, see the epilogue in my book *Revolution!* (Billerica, Mass.: Discipleship Publications International, 1998) 203-7.

is with young children. His charges knew so little about the ministry that he basically spoon-fed them, and they responded well to such leading, for it was absolutely required at that stage. Added to the equation was the fact that the older members in these lukewarm churches possessed distorted views of discipleship, making their views the least trustworthy. Trust in older leaders or in a team of leaders were foreign concepts in that setting, and the residual effects of that unfortunate combination have not been easy to eliminate.

As campus converts matured and perhaps became a part of the church ministry staff, they began having their own ideas about what should be done in the ministry. However, they managed to remain reasonably patient by looking forward to the day when they had their own groups to lead and could then call the shots. Add five or ten years to this scenario in older, larger churches, and some significant problems have ensued. Once these people reach the peak of their leadership potential and do not become the top leaders of their groups, their morale is destined to take a serious nosedive—unless they are made to feel like a valuable part of a leadership team in which their input is sought out, respected and valued. If we do not adopt the team leadership approach, the consequences will be neither positive nor minor.

Biblical Team Leaders

I want to share two examples of Biblical leaders who understood the team leadership approach: David of the first kingdom and the Messianic David of our present kingdom. First, look at David's leadership style. He knew the importance of enlisting the advice and support of his leaders, as well as those in the lowest ranks. Read the following excerpt from 1 Chronicles 13 carefully, for it contains a great example of building team:

> David conferred with each of his officers, the commanders of thousands and commanders of hundreds. He then said to the

> whole assembly of Israel, "If it seems good to you and if it is
> the will of the LORD our God, let us send word far and wide to
> the rest of our brothers throughout the territories of Israel, and
> also to the priests and Levites who are with them in their towns
> and pasturelands, to come and join us. Let us bring the ark of
> our God back to us, for we did not inquire of it during the reign
> of Saul." The whole assembly agreed to do this, because it
> seemed right to all the people. (1 Chronicles 13:1-4)

The people had always been drawn to David because he was a true leader—one who led the troops into battle himself. He did not simply direct them into it. However, he shared the glory with his key men, as the remainder of that chapter demonstrates powerfully. Great leaders give those under their charge all the credit when things go well and take all the responsibility when things go badly. (Read that last sentence again to make sure you got it!)

Second, look at the example of Jesus, the only perfect leader who ever walked on planet Earth. He knew how to engage the hearts and the loyalty of his key leaders. As disciples age in the Lord, they must be led in an age-appropriate manner, which demands more of a team approach. Neither our children nor God's children will respond well to being treated like five-year-olds when they are fifteen.

Jesus understood and implemented this principle wonderfully. In John 13:13 he said, "You call me 'Teacher' and 'Lord,' and rightly so, for that is what I am." However, he later recognized their growing maturity and his changing relationship with them:

> "I no longer call you servants, because a servant does not
> know his master's business. Instead, I have called you
> friends, for everything that I learned from my Father I have
> made known to you." (John 15:15)

In other words, he was no longer doing all of the thinking and planning independently, but pulling them into "everything" that was a part of God's plan for them. The end result was that they were willing to do anything to carry out that plan, including dying as martyrs. After they had been taught his and his Father's convictions, Jesus both valued and trusted them to be a circle of friends, collectively leading the ministry.

Building Team

Bottom line, a great and decisive leader is not one who has all the best ideas and who makes all the decisions as the top leader. He just initiates the process of making decisions, rallying around him those who are going to be responsible for implementing them. He leads the discussions and makes the final decision after getting the best input possible. Then those he leads will gladly fight to implement the decisions, knowing that the decisions are theirs as well—and in the event of failure, they will not be guilty of blameshifting. It will be a team effort. But rest assured that employing consensus techniques only to placate those under your leadership will not ultimately satisfy them, because they will perceive your true motives.

Being decisive does not mean that you make all of the decisions, but rather that you determine the *process* by which they will be made and then gain others' understanding and approval of the process. A marriage plaque in our home reads thus: "The goal of marriage is not to think alike; it is to think together." A great leader welcomes the opinions of others because it broadens his knowledge of the subject under consideration, and he relishes strong personalities around him who question his opinions. Such a leader looks for the opportunity to make others feel heard and therefore valuable to the relationship. This is team leadership—most aptly described as Golden Rule leadership. If you thought that the greatness of being a high-level leader is in being able to call more shots yourself, you are going to be ineffective at best and downright dangerous at worst. Randy McKean recently asked those in our leadership group to read a book that I think should be must reading for every person on the ministry staff of every church. The book is entitled *The Habits of Highly Effective Churches*, written by George Barna. Barna leads a research team that studies churches of all kinds across America, so that his writing is not simply an airing of his pet opinions, but the result of broad research. His conclusions about leadership-style could not be clearer.

> One of the most amazing revelations from my research was that in the typical church, the pastor is intimately involved in most, if not all, of the ministry's decisions. (Yes, *control* is a major problem in the typical American church.) In the highly effective churches, however, the leader-pastor has the final say on all of the major ministry decisions, but is literally uninvolved in the vast majority of decisions made in the ministry.[2]

As you read this intriguing book, you will be struck by the fact that the most effective leaders lay a threefold foundation of leadership: building team, raising up new leaders (including many not on staff—"lay leaders," he calls them) and then allowing all these leaders to innovate in ways that are meaningful both to them as individuals and to the ministry as a whole.

Before we close the chapter, some self-examination of your leadership is in order. Ask yourself the following questions, and struggle to be honest with your answers. When you finish, ask those whom you lead to honestly answer these questions about you. If you will do this exercise, you will be well on your way to developing an accurate understanding of your leadership style, and from that vantage point, growth becomes an exciting possibility.

- Do you feel threatened when your opinions are questioned by those whom you lead?

[2]George Barna, *The Habits of Highly Effective Churches* (Ventura, Calif.: Regal Books, 1999) 51.

- Do you feel that others are disloyal to you if they question your opinions?
- When you do not have the opportunity to pull others into the decision-making process, does this leave you feeling unsettled, or do you feel relieved that you can now make the decision without interference?
- Do those whom you lead feel valued?
- Do you often seek input from those you lead about the way that you lead?
- Would others describe you as a model of humility or as a person who thinks he is just about always right?
- Do you find that younger disciples and leaders think you are much more awesome than older disciples and leaders seem to think you are?

The answers to these questions say a lot about whether you are a controlling leader or a team leader. Therefore, leadership is far more than telling others what to do—it is leading in a Biblical manner, thus eliciting full-hearted participation and subsequent appreciation for you as a Christlike leader. Let's be great and let's be decisive, but let's be very sure that we understand what this really means!

6

Team Leadership
The Practicals

S

Prayerfully, earlier chapters of this book have challenged your model of leadership and inspired an excitement about developing, participating in and contributing as a disciple to your own leadership teams. I say "teams" because there are multiple applications of Golden Rule leadership that all disciples can benefit from and find applications for in their own lives. Husbands and fathers need to consider how they lead their marriages and families; wives and mothers need to consider how they lead in the roles God uniquely equipped them for in the family, church and community. Whether male or female, we each have the opportunity, privilege and responsibility to be on God's teams as leaders, contributors and benefactors in fulfilling his vision for the body of Christ.

These teams are currently found among us in at least the following structures: singles households, families, family groups, Bible talks, ministry staffs and leadership groups at every level of church organization.

> It was he who gave some to be apostles, some to be prophets, some to be evangelists, and some to be pastors and teachers, to prepare God's people for works of service, so that the body of Christ may be built up until we all reach unity in the faith and in the knowledge of the Son of God and become mature, attaining to the whole measure of the fullness of Christ.
>
> Then we will no longer be infants, tossed back and forth by the waves, and blown here and there by every wind of teaching and by the cunning and craftiness of men in their

deceitful scheming. Instead, speaking the truth in love, we
will in all things grow up into him who is the Head, that is,
Christ. From him the whole body, joined and held together by
every supporting ligament, grows and builds itself up in love,
as each part does its work. (Ephesians 4:11-16)

Paul defines the Biblical application of team for the church.
We are to become a united, spiritual group, fulfilling the mission
of Jesus. That mission is to show the world the Father and to
love one another as Jesus loved, to make disciples of all nations,
thus bringing glory to God in every generation. Each of us who
is a faithful disciple is in one or more of the team situations I
mentioned. The operative phrase in creating team is "the whole
body...grows and builds itself up in love, as each part does its
work" (v16). God's vision is that every part of his team con-
tributes to and benefits from the growth of the whole group, as
each part builds up the team out of love.

I am convinced from numerous current discussions and
events that God is powerfully moving us toward a new understanding and better practice of his word in this area. God's revelation never changes—but our understanding does, as we are
moved by his Spirit through both the best and worst of what we
have been doing. We have hit some walls of unhappiness and
dissatisfaction among our disciples, and our leaders are experiencing undue strain and a lack of motivation, especially those
in sector and region leadership. I believe both of these maladies
can be solved by growth in the practice of Golden Rule leadership so that each team of disciples is being built up in love, having their own needs met, sharing the load of Biblical
responsibility so life is not just bearable but truly abundant and
therefore, glorifying to God. When God is glorified, he will
make things grow in exciting and unprecedented ways.

We must ensure that the excitement, joy and satisfaction of
living the Jesus life is being experienced by every part of God's
team. For example, the best advertisement for any sport is

people who love playing the game. So it is with Jesus. When he is good news to disciples, outsiders want to join such a happy, fulfilled team. This sounds like the abundant, "rest for your souls" (Matthew 11:29) and blessed lifestyle promised to us in the Bible.

I was converted to such a team. I loved being on it and loved my teammates. Evangelism was simply telling others to come and see what I had found, and the attractiveness and love of the team mostly did the rest. It should still be this way on every kingdom team from the groups that carry the greatest load of responsibility to those who just began and are the least experienced. Jesus came to carry our sorrows, light up our lives and teach us how to do the same for each other. May God's teams begin anew with fresh vision, fresh love and fresh motivation, because we are on Jesus' heaven-bound team!

Jesus' Vision for Team

Building team begins by defining what kind of team we will be and what we want to accomplish. You can build a new team spirit into an old team (new coaches do this all the time) or build a new team, spirit and all. I believe we need some of both in many of our current ministry groups. The key is found in what you aim for and how you build it.

Just before I wrote this chapter, Chip Mitchell, who leads our campus ministries in Boston, preached a great sermon after a leadership retreat. On the retreat, Randy McKean had presented an incredibly refreshing perspective from Scripture on motivation and building our spiritual teams for the next ten years. Chip incorporated and expanded on this from John 12-15. The theme of both evangelists was that every disciple and team of disciples needs to focus on God, Jesus, loving each other and going to heaven. Chip pointed out that repeatedly in the last days of Jesus' life, recorded by John, Jesus focused on glorifying God, going to God and leading the disciples to the Father (John 12:23-27). He focused his disciples on loving each other and on glorifying God (John 13:1-17, 34-35). He also taught them not to worry about troubling matters on earth, but to focus on what is prepared in heaven, on being with him and the Father, and on having Jesus' peace in the midst of trouble (John 14:1-31).

Chip concluded by taking us to John 15. Jesus was about to leave his disciples. They were scared, faithless and discouraged. Jesus' message essentially was, *Abide in me and the Father. Stay connected to me and let these words I have just spoken about God, the Son of God, loving each other and going to heaven be what you focus on, and you will bear fruit that will last. People will be drawn to your team of joy, peace, love and excitement about heaven.* This team-building with God, Jesus and each other will create a compelling impact on others invited into it and draw them to Jesus as he is given credit for producing it. Jesus did not scare the disciples into evangelism with the threat of being pruned. Rather he is saying that as we abide in him and his words abide in us, our character will be changed by our connection with him and the Father and our obedience to the truth. He encouraged them with the good news that if they would stay focused on God, Jesus, heaven and loving each other, growth would result from such a healthy, happy team. This is why in John 14:27, he says,

> "Peace I leave with you; my peace I give you. I do not give to you as the world gives. Do not let your hearts be troubled and do not be afraid."

Too many evangelists in older churches are troubled and afraid—afraid of staff meetings and statistic sheets and discipleship groups. Too many family group leaders are troubled and afraid that they cannot motivate their groups to produce what the evangelists want. Too many disciples are troubled and afraid—afraid of campaigns and pushes and workshops. Jesus' last words essentially were, *Do not be afraid, and do not let your hearts be troubled. Trust in God, trust also in me. Love each other and keep looking forward to heaven with us all. Then you will bear much fruit, fruit that will last and is to my Father's glory.* This is what every team in our churches must aim for and build toward. Happy and healthy teams will grow to the glory of God!

Defining and Training Team Leadership

Effective team leaders recognize the importance and value of each person on the team, and they seek to make each person feel important and valuable. In Romans 12 and 1 Corinthians 12, Paul exalts the value of diversity and the importance of the weaker parts. Everyone is uniquely special to God and must be made to feel that way on God's team—or we have failed in Golden Rule leadership. It is clear from the way too many among us are feeling that we have failed in some ways that now need to be joyfully corrected. Great leaders are decisive about the right things—the important and godly—not the urgent and shortsighted.

Starting with our families, singles households and family groups, we must deliberately design leadership that facilitates everyone feeling valued and vitally important. We must move on to every family group leader, intern, sector leader, region leader and top leadership group. We must treat each one as we would want to be treated, according to God's vision for the team. When each of these groups is led in a godly way and each disciple feels like a valued part of God's team (at whatever level), our people will be happy, healthy and bearing fruit to God's glory.

This means training leaders to think from the perspective of those being led more than from their own perspective. Good parents think about what is best for the children in training them to grow up to be healthy and productive. Golden Rule leaders think about what is best for the people being led, while we all work together to accomplish God's vision. This means that meetings for staff and family group leaders should focus on the needs that those leaders have in creating a happy, healthy team with each *unique* group of people they lead.

Dean and Kim Farmer from Berlin, who lead one of the ten fastest growing first-world churches, shared at a leadership retreat how they have learned to focus on having specific victories at each step of the team-building process, rather than just focusing on a final result. This means encouraging and coaching tough team situations through to small victories until in time, they see the more tangible and celebrated baptisms and numerical victories of health and growth.

By emphasizing end results, we sometimes hit those who are struggling the most with one more measurement of their failures. Then we wonder why they quit leading or why those who watch or hear about such leadership do not want to lead. We must see this for what it is. People want to know that you are on their side, helping them win, not on their case because they are losing. Dean and Kim are harvesting the healthy result of Golden Rule leadership.

Developing Top Leadership Groups

One of the most encouraging things in my life is being in Randy McKean's discipleship group for the New England and Europe world sector of our churches. I praise God for where God has set my boundaries (Psalm 16:6) and for the companions who share them with me in the Lord. Randy has grown in developing a team leadership around him. It consists of the elders and world sector administrator as his *oversight* group, the geographic sector leaders as his *influence group* and the regional church leaders as his *input group*. (The exact terms we use are not so important, but the defining of the function of the groups is essential.) We have wrestled with how elders and evangelists work together and have forged a great balance of mutual respect and submission to the collective wisdom of the oversight group.

Randy had the most to lose and to gain by choosing this model of leadership. He stood to lose control and efficiency, but stood to gain better judgment, better morale, better allocation of responsibility and less personal strain. Jethro, in Exodus 18:21-23, gave Moses timeless leadership advice when he addressed the dissatisfaction of the people and the simultaneous strain on the leaders as an organizational problem. Our people have too often gone home dissatisfied, and our leaders have shown too many signs of stress and of not standing the strain. God is moving us to a new model. Randy has been a great example of making the "faith move" to a more satisfying and less stressful leadership model. What about the way you lead? Change is so vital if we are to keep growing and allowing God's Spirit to mature and lead us.

In shaping our group, we all recognize that more than one strong personality and opinion leader can and must share the privilege and responsibility of leading a large and complex organization like a church—and especially a world sector. It is good and essential to have independent thinkers to evaluate and contribute to difficult and often high-impact decisions. Diversity of strengths and weaknesses, gifts, talents and personality types help us to relate to more of those who are led. Such diversity of leaders can better anticipate pitfalls or opportunities as they look at the same set of facts and issues.

We in Randy's group have all bought into the conviction that team leadership is most likely to be right most often. Defining a new mode of operation and having a unified commitment to it is critical for team leadership to work. We still must catch ourselves when we slip back into old habits, but conviction leads to new and better patterns of leading. It is an evolution led by the Spirit and fueled by faith, hope, love and experience. Our goal is to see similar leadership groups formed in every region and church in our world sector. We are committed to seeing

Golden Rule leadership implemented down to the smallest and newest of God's teams under our care and charge!

Distinct Roles

Beyond sharing equal conviction about team leadership, groups must have well-defined roles and operational dynamics. Currently, we are further along in defining roles than operational dynamics. Randy has done a great job of assessing who does what best and assigning tasks accordingly. Gordon is our teacher and overseer of European church needs. He and Theresa have great counseling and nurturing skills, along with a depth of Bible knowledge. Jeanie and I have been assigned oversight of our HOPE work and Spiritual Recovery ministries. Dan is our administrator and our finance and organizational expert. The geographic sector leaders and region leaders obviously have their specific ministry responsibilities. These roles have been defined, not on the basis of simply friendship and historic relationships, though we have those, but more out of a recognition of God-given qualifications and unique capabilities.

With our encouragement, Randy and Kay agreed not to take on any specific leadership within the world sector. Instead, they orchestrate strategy that produces healthy disciples and includes the necessary training in every world sector ministry. We have come to agree with the observation made by George Barna:

> If you study the leaders described in the Bible, you soon discover that every great leader called by God worked with a strong team of ministry associates. The fact that churches are now embracing a leader-led, multiple-person, team-based ministry is exciting and certainly bodes well for the future....[1]

We want Randy and Kay ultimately to macromanage the world sector and to be the change-agents to see that the Biblical

---

[1] George Barna, *The Habits of Highly Effective Churches* (Ventura, Calif.: Regal Books, 1999) 37.

vision and ingredients that produce happy, healthy and productive disciples reach every part of our world sector. If Randy's group models these dynamics, then they can be taught by training and imitation to every other leadership group. People are happier and more productive when roles are well defined—even if a role is not their first choice. We have tried to assign roles primarily by people's need and by their unique qualifications. Again Barna speaks to our need to understand the multiple benefits of team:

> Teams are useful when there is mutual dependence among the members because they understand that their cooperation creates synergy: they can accomplish more by working together than by solo.[2]

One disciple cannot create all the necessary movement in terms of motivation, knowledge or application, but together God's team of disciples can.

Operational Dynamics

Once the people and roles have been decided, it is important to agree on how the group will operate when it is together. Our basic dynamics could be summed up in the following way:

1. *Individuals must accept their own personal responsibility in the group, including the following:*
   - submission to the unity of the group—simply following the practice of the Kip McKeans, Bairds and Gempels while they were leading the Boston church that we only move forward if all in the decision-making group agree. Otherwise we assume that God is trying to teach all or one of us something through the discussion and process
   - awareness of our own strengths and weaknesses—both of which are acknowledged and addressed freely by the group
   - openness with our own sins—each seeking discipling and personal input from the group

[2]Barna, 54.

- vulnerability with our burdens and needs—so that the group can provide collective strength and renewal
- commitment to bowing out of personally sentimental decisions if it's deemed best by the group
- faith in God to work through or in spite of group decisions (Proverbs 16:3)

2. *The goals of the group process must be understood.*

At a recent meeting of our leadership group, Randy gave a simple summary of the way we need to approach decisions:

- work out the philosophy and overall direction for evangelization and spiritual growth in the world sector
- gather information for the communication and organization needed to produce and maintain unity as we grow the world sector
- make the decisions needed, as dictated by these first two goals, and then delegate responsibility and a process of accountability to see that they happen in an orderly and consistent fashion

Certainly team leadership can be difficult, and we have had our struggles, differences and walls of resistance. I have come to see the following as frequent obstacles to the development of team:

- the team concept is not agreed to at an emotional level by any one member of the group
- control is more valued than team by any individual member of the team
- sincere differences of conviction or opinion remain unreconciled, putting unity at stake
- no defined process or not enough time set aside for arriving at team decisions or for developing team dynamics

- the group is too large to effectively discuss issues or build family in a timely fashion

Success in team leadership can be defined in the following ways:

- those led by the group are healthy, happy and fruitful disciples
- those led by the group trust the collective wisdom of the leadership and feel secure about following them
- those within the leadership team feel valued and free to express convictions, opinions, reservations, questions or disagreements while still being accepted by the group
- the Biblical goals of the group are achieved over a period of time
- decisions can be arrived at in an atmosphere of honesty, integrity, respect and safety
- unity is maintained in spite of disagreement

As Gordon has already warned, one of the great temptations in reading this will be for leaders to assume they are already practicing what we are describing. A second would be to assume that by announcing your intent to move in this direction you have significantly changed the way it has been. We have found that *defining team leadership is much easier than practicing it,* and we see ourselves much more as a work in progress than as having arrived at any final destination. Philippians 1:25-26 best describes my intent for this book and its impact:

> Convinced of this, I know that [it] will remain, and [it] will continue with all of [us] for [our] progress and joy in the faith, so that through [it] being with [us] again [our] joy in Christ Jesus will overflow on account of [it]. (adapted)

I am personally grateful to God for where he has brought me as a disciple and leader. I am writing this in the New Hampshire woods by a lake, where today I had a great quiet time. I began by reading Psalm 85, and verses 6-13 especially caught my heart and emotions:

> Will you not revive us again,
>   that your people may rejoice in you?
> Show us your unfailing love, O LORD,
>   and grant us your salvation.
>
> I will listen to what God the LORD will say;
>   he promises peace to his people, his saints—
>   but let them not return to folly.
> Surely his salvation is near those who fear him,
>   that his glory may dwell in our land.
>
> Love and faithfulness meet together;
>   righteousness and peace kiss each other.
> Faithfulness springs forth from the earth,
>   and righteousness looks down from heaven.
> The LORD will indeed give what is good,
>   and our land will yield its harvest.
> Righteousness goes before him
>   and prepares the way for his steps. (Psalm 85:6-13)

First, I was struck by the psalmist's question, "Will you not revive us again, that your people may rejoice in you?" I have asked, *Why aren't our people more happy?* I believe our "system" of ministry has sometimes inadvertently developed into that which robs our joy more than it facilitates ways for people to rejoice in God. The writer says, "I will listen to what God the Lord will say; he promises peace to his people, his saints—but let them not return to folly." I believe we are on the verge of reclaiming God's promises of peace to his saints and of his reviving us again!

I love what the psalm says from there (bracketed comments are mine):

> Surely his salvation is near those who fear him,
>   that his glory may dwell in our land.
> Love and faithfulness meet together;
>   righteousness and peace kiss each other.
> Faithfulness springs forth from the earth *[God's
>   happy, healthy teams of disciples]*,
>   and righteousness looks down from heaven *[where we
>   are headed]*.
> The LORD will indeed give what is good *[happiness,
>   love, peace]*,
>   and our land will yield its harvest *[fruit that
>   lasts, added to already healthy teams of disciples]*.
> Righteousness goes before him
>   and prepares the way for his steps. (Psalm 85:9-13)

God is leading us to take great steps forward. Let us be sure to have righteous hearts before him as he produces healthy teams of disciples through Golden Rule leadership. Winning and keeping as many disciples as possible will always be a battle, but when we lead, love and follow together, as teams of God's children, he will see us through every challenge to eternal victory.

7

Leadership Relationships
Elders and Evangelists
Part One: The Roles

S

Central to the discussion of leadership in the kingdom of God and building team is the relationship between elders and evangelists. Certainly both roles trace back to forerunners in Old Testament times—prophets, priests, wise men, patriarchs and judges. To these roots and illustrations we can add the specific qualifications, teachings and examples about both roles from the New Testament, thus gaining a reliable composite of the elements that should be found in both evangelists and elders in today's church.

Maturing Churches

I do not think that there would be much argument in the International Churches of Christ about the fact that we have focused more on defining and developing the role of evangelists than elders. Almost certainly this is because many of our roots have been in campus ministries, and we are just beginning to have significant numbers of disciples who are old enough to have believing children, a primary qualification for an elder. Also, in our beginnings we built many new churches in which one-couple leadership teams planted small groups of young, mobile disciples in many cities of the world. Training tended to focus on evangelism, discipling, Bible knowledge, preaching and rapid growth. As Al Baird has put it, we were in "aircraft carrier mode," launching many small churches as fast as possible to evangelize the world in our generation.

Now, two to three decades later, as disciples and their families mature, we are beginning to see more elders appointed. As such men and their wives seek to take their place beside evangelists and women's ministry leaders, it is imperative to forge a great understanding of these roles and how they work together. We need to see great examples of elder and evangelist leadership teams.

Vital Unity

The marriage of the roles of elder and evangelist is crucial for many reasons. The church is primarily a family, and in a family the relationship that Mom and Dad have is the emotional and relational model for the children. If Mom and Dad are divided and fighting for their selfish interests, so will the family be. If elders and evangelists are fighting for control or personal agendas, God's family will be insecure and unhappy and will imitate all the wrong character traits. Conversely, if elders and evangelists exhibit Christlike character, mutual love and respect, and joyful fulfillment of their God-given roles in the church, God's plan works. It is not difficult to decide which kind of marriage or family we would rather be in!

It takes no less effort to build great elder and evangelist relationships than it does great marriages. There are no short-cuts, but the rewards for everyone are more than worth the effort! This means both elders and evangelists need to appreciate one anothers' roles, worth and place. As in marriage, they must love, honor and respect each other with a sincere desire to grow in all aspects of the relationship. With these attitudes in place, mutual joy, satisfaction and a mature family will emerge in time as God makes things grow.

Our goal is to help disciples build better leadership teams throughout the whole church, from the most basic ministry group to world sector leadership. Elders and evangelists, because of their profile, example and decision making, are crucial pacesetters for all disciples to imitate. This is why I believe all disciples can benefit from reading the qualifications for leaders and how they should work together. It should give disciples a frame of reference for how their present leaders are doing and show each disciple the spiritual qualities and vision all should aim for so God can better use us. We will not all be elders or evangelists, but we all need to understand the roles, their purpose and how God intends for people to work together on his team.

Qualifications and Responsibilities of Evangelists

The word "evangelist" derives its meaning from the concept of a herald, one who proclaims good news. In ancient times it connoted the idea of one who brought word of victory from a faraway battlefield—where life and death, slavery and freedom, were hanging in the balance. It is this image that Paul has in mind when he quotes Isaiah in Romans 10:15: "How beautiful are the feet of those who bring good news!" So the evangelist brings word of victory, of freedom—of life, not death. He reports from the spiritual battlefield where Jesus has defeated Satan and declared all his disciples to be winners. Paul is specific about the qualities and responsibilities of evangelists in 1 Timothy, 2 Timothy and Titus, in which he writes to young evangelists about how to do their job.

Apprenticeship (2 Timothy 3:10-11)

Paul decided to disciple Timothy after Timothy excelled as a young convert (Acts 16:1-3). He traveled with Paul and learned his way of life, how he taught and how he led both unbelievers to faith and new converts to being strengthened and established in the faith. From this backdrop of experience, of being with him, Paul wrote letters to Timothy about specific tasks and roles for him to fulfill in the churches where he was on his own.

I am very thankful to the evangelists who gave me on-the-job discipling and training. While I was a student at the

University of Florida, Sam Laing baptized and inspired me by his life to want to be an evangelist. I will never forget the way I watched with eager eyes and listened to every Bible talk, every conversation with non-Christians or new converts, every sermon or training class for points of reference and imitation for when I would be on my own. I continued to learn from Kip McKean, Tom Brown and Al Baird. I am learning still from Randy McKean in Boston. There is no substitute for walking with others to learn the ministry.

Example (1 Timothy 4:12)

Setting an example in speech, life, love, faith and purity are character prerequisites for becoming an evangelist. Jesus condemned hypocritical leaders, and Paul identifies areas of example most needing attention, especially in young evangelists. It should also be noted that while Timothy was "young," young in those days probably meant he was in his thirties. To be exemplary in these areas still takes time and development, regardless of talent, heart and training.

While I understand the urgency and inspiration of raising up young leaders, I also believe we must guard against confusing a cosmetic appearance of maturity with the genuine article—only grown over time. It should not take forever to raise up an evangelist, and we err when some ministry veterans are without that designation because of our neglect. But perhaps we have erred more often by placing the mantle on some before their time. Profile and pressure are tests of anyone's character. I am for having campus interns and getting young disciples into leadership training, but let's be careful not to ruin the horses before we get much racing out of them. For example, they should run on smaller tracks with lesser stakes before racing at the Kentucky Derby. As further protection, the older veteran, Paul, still gave younger evangelists much direction and guidance, even as they led.

Public Scripture Reading (1 Timothy 4:13)

Scripture has a sacred place in God's plan for his church. The pages and letters are not themselves holy, but the truths that will have impact on minds and hearts are. Evangelists are to devote themselves to public Scripture reading. I grew up going to Bible Memory Camp, in which we received a week of free summer camp for memorizing fifty to one hundred portions of Scripture of one to five verses each. Later, as a young disciple, I took Acts, Romans and Spiritual Training classes in which scripture memory was expected, enjoyed and treasured. While it seems I have less capacity to memorize now, I can still recall portions of those scriptures and where many of them are located in the Bible.

Each summer I lead a section of the HOPE Youth Corps, consisting of thirty-five to forty college-age and teen disciples. Though these are some of the church's stronger young disciples spiritually, when recently I asked for Scripture to be quoted at a fireside devotional, no one could quote even a favorite scripture, much less a topically appropriate one. I bring this up because I believe it is symptomatic of the need we have for evangelists to publicly profile the Scriptures and to inspire the personal valuing and the retaining of them in our hearts. The responses to a request for popular song lyrics, movie titles or sports team records would provide an interesting comparison of values.

Preaching (2 Timothy 4:1-2)

Paul's most passionate mandate to the evangelist is to preach the word of God. He is to do this with a full understanding of the eternal stakes for both preacher and hearer. Scripture is to be the content. Readiness, patience and carefulness are to be the accompanying tools for God's workman to whom the gospel and men's souls have been entrusted. The older I become, the more I see the significance of this responsibility. The patience and carefulness ring louder and more meaningfully than when I was younger. The emphasis of and pattern of an evangelist's preaching should be carefully guarded and watched to ensure that they are providing a spiritual diet consisting of healthy or sound teaching.

All too often, we measure sermons too singularly, according to how powerful, fiery or animated they are. We would do well to examine how carefully constructed and seasoned with patience they are. Our preaching must reflect a commitment to building God's way. Otherwise, the results will not be lasting. Medically speaking, low cholesterol, long life and wellness are urgent priorities, but fast food, the right pills or quick fixes cannot attain these. Spiritually speaking, salvation, eternity and character development are urgent and of the highest priority, but we will be not be successful in finding them via shortcuts. Our preaching must correct, rebuke and encourage a godly lifestyle that is first of all livable. Second, it is to be good news, and third, it must be recommendable to others.

Teaching (1 Timothy 4:13)

Along with public Scripture reading and preaching, the evangelist is to teach. Teaching can be distinguished from preaching in that it is more systematic and thorough, taking time for detail and for giving a solid framework about God's revelation of his will. Evangelists are responsible to see that settings and curriculums are in place that will give God's people both the milk and meat of the Bible (Hebrews 5:12-14). We must expect disciples to be willing to be taught, and evangelists must insist on the personal responsibility of each disciple to engage in a learning process with measurable results.

Appointments (Titus 1:5; 1 Timothy 5:17-25)

In Titus 1 Paul says he left Titus to appoint elders in every town where churches had been planted. Evangelists are responsible not only for appointments, but for raising up disciples to meet the specific qualifications given for deacons, elders and their wives. Why else would they be given the qualifications and then told to appoint people?

In 1 Timothy 5, Paul warns the young, inexperienced Timothy to both honor elders (appointees) who do well with their responsibilities and to not be hasty to lay hands on (appoint) others until their characters have been further revealed. Not being hasty implies that time is one of the great tests of what is behind the mask of any human being. We can only see what shows. Time and God, Paul says, will pass judgment on the good or bad of our hearts and characters.

Expectations (1 Timothy 3:14-16)

Evangelists are to hold out God's expectations to those belonging to his family. There is a code of conduct for disciples consistent with the heart and character of the living God we serve. Just as Joshua and all good heads of households have an "as for me and my house" code (Joshua 24:15), so God has a code for the church. Chapters 4, 5 and 6 of 1 Timothy lay out God's expectations for many things, ranging from food to dealing with gossip, slander and quarrels—and for many groups of people, from elders to widows to the rich.

Heart, Goals and Nature (1 Timothy 1:2-5, 15-17; 2:3-6; 3:16; Titus 2:11-14)

When Paul writes to Timothy, he constantly reminds him of God's heart, goals and nature, for communicating these are the ultimate measurements and keys of an evangelist's success. He must show people God. He must know God and get his people to know God. He must keep God's glory and goals at the forefront of all he does and all his people do.

In the above passages Paul identifies a number of truths that evangelists need to show to their people. God "wants all men to be saved and to come to a knowledge of the truth." In light of this reality, evangelists must both call for an evangelistic fervor and lead the charge in term of evangelistic example.

"Jesus came into the world to save sinners." Jesus has "unlimited patience" so that even the worst sinner can be saved. Also, "there is one God and one mediator between God and man, the man Jesus Christ." Jesus came to the earth in bodily form, was seen, preached, believed in and taken back to heaven.

The evangelist is a servant of his God and of God's people. He is one who knows both and keeps them connected in knowledge, spirit and action through his preaching and example.

Heaven (2 Timothy 4:6-8)

Paul wants evangelists to look forward to heaven and to teach their people that all who love Jesus will meet there for our reward. We must fight the fight, run the race and keep the faith, for it is all headed somewhere—a place better than what the eye has seen, the ear has heard or anything that has entered into the heart of man. I have seen, heard and imagined a lot of great places and things in my life, but heaven will make them all pale in comparison. Evangelists must keep the wonder of heaven in view as we all face the challenges of being godly on earth. Focusing on heaven sustains the divine perspective!

Qualifications and Responsibilities of Elders

Not long before this writing, Jim Blough, elder for the Washington D.C. church and Commonwealth world sector, taught a lesson on the role of elders for a kingdom elders' retreat held in Colorado. It was one of the best lessons I have ever heard outlining the Biblical role. I will simply reiterate the gist of what Jim taught and add some of my thoughts where appropriate.

Elders have been present throughout history and have been a part of God's plan from Exodus to Revelation. They are cited for their failures by prophets such as Isaiah and Ezekiel and seen as contributors to the problem of hypocrisy in Jewish leadership during Jesus' ministry. However, the New Testament closes in Revelation with twenty-four elders leading worship in heaven, pointing to God's intention that there be men worthy of respect, held up for having lived righteously for longer than most.

Elders are meant to be mature men, well respected because of their success in family and life. They are to be trusted advisors because of their seasoned wisdom, incorruptible and just character and lack of personal agendas in the affairs of the community. Various terms are used to describe different aspects of their role in the Bible. "Bishop," "overseer" and "presbyter" refer primarily to their leadership and authority functions. "Elder," "shepherd" and "pastor" refer primarily to their maturity and nurturing qualities.

Paul enumerates specific qualifications for elders in 1 Timothy and Titus. Since they are nearly identical, I will quote 1 Timothy 3:1-7:

> Here is a trustworthy saying: If anyone sets his heart on being an overseer, he desires a noble task. Now the overseer must be above reproach, the husband of but one wife, temperate, self-controlled, respectable, hospitable, able to teach, not given to drunkenness, not violent but gentle, not quarrelsome, not a lover of money. He must manage his own family well and see that his children obey him with proper respect. (If anyone does not know how to manage his own family, how can he take care of God's church?) He must not be a recent convert, or he may become conceited and fall under the same judgment as the devil. He must also have a good reputation with outsiders, so that he will not fall into disgrace and into the devil's trap.

It should be noted that the character traits called for in elders are also called for from all disciples generally in Scripture. Elders are just expected to be further along at exhibiting mature Christian qualities more of the time. They are to be older in life experience and as disciples, not being new converts who would let the profile of the role make them conceited.

Success at training children to become disciples provides a living exhibit of what younger Christian families are aiming for and serves as evidence that a man can be trusted to manage God's church (v5). I have spent much time meditating on why God uses family spirituality as such a significant and pointed qualifier for leading his people. Clearly, he sees this as a fundamental test of the qualities needed for the more challenging task of leading the church. Leading a family to spiritual conviction and practice requires exemplifying our discipleship up close and personal with uniquely diverse individuals who know our sins, weaknesses, defeats and victories over time. We have long preached "as goes the family, so goes the ministry" about our leadership. We can rest assured that one will reflect the other and vice versa. Many evangelists have not currently been tested in this area because their children are still young, but it should be an aim for all who lead in God's church.

When there are men who reasonably meet these qualifications, what then is the value of their role as elders? Looking at both the Old Testament and the New Testament, at least seven functions can be found that were needed then and are still needed now.

Overseeing and Managing the Church (1 Timothy 3:1-7, Acts 20:28-31)

Both of these passages indicate responsibility for the overall welfare and health of the church. Elders are to keep watch for the doctrinal soundness of what is taught and the personal application by each disciple. They are to prevent internal disruption of godly living by either leaders or members and, as they did with their own families, see that every part does its work, gets its needs met and ultimately stays spiritually healthy. They have responsibility and authority to see that the integrity and spirituality of both the individual and collective whole are protected and maintained.

Advising Leaders *(Exodus 18:2-27)*

Jethro, Moses' father-in-law, gave great leadership consulting to Moses. Moses was zealously trying to serve God and to lead the people—and thought he was doing a great job of it! As Jim Blough put it, "Everything always looks and sounds great from the pulpit." However, Jethro stood with the people, as elders do, and saw many needs not being met; he was then able to advise Moses on how to better respond to these needs.

In 1 Kings 12:1-19 the elders gave better advice than the young men because they were concerned about the well-being *of the people.* The young men were concerned about pleasing *the king* because they "had grown up with him and were serving him." The elders had lived life over two kingships and had a long-term perspective that was clearer.

Preserving Unity *(Deuteronomy 19:11-12, 21:18-20, 22:13-18)*

Three types of conflict resolution are seen in Deuteronomy. There were justice issues between towns, children rebelling against parents and marriage problems. There are many areas of potential conflict in the kingdom today. Men who are considered fair, of high integrity, unbiased and knowledgeable in the Scriptures are often in demand for settling disputes. We have all needed and will continue to need help with conflict resolution. It is not a matter of whether, but of when.

Setting an Example *(1 Peter 4:1-4)*

Elders provide a model of the complete spiritual package in character, family management, and loving God and people. They show that Christians can live healthy, happy and fruitful lives in all areas of godly living. Yet they are not show-offs, lording their success over others, but servants willingly offering their spiritual experience to those in need of it.

Protecting the Flock *(Acts 20:25-31, Ezekiel 34:15-16)*

First by watching themselves, elders are vigilant to spot the ways that ungodly habits, attitudes and ways of life sneak into the church. They are able to refute false teaching from within or without. They take care of strong and weak alike, seeing to it that they lovingly live with each other.

Meeting Specific Needs (James 5:13-16; Acts 11:27-30, 16:1-5; Judges 21:15-23; Esther 1:13-2:4)

Some specific needs that were met by elders in the Bible include anointing the sick, administering benevolence, making special church announcements, finding wives for the brothers and giving advice.

Providing Security (Hebrews 13:7)

Elders have lives whose outcome is testimony that God's will is good, pleasing and acceptable—it works. They can share about short-term failures but demonstrate long-term victory. People are to imitate not the outcome of their lives, but their faith, which holds promise and the key to a successful outcome for all. It is amazing how people love to hear about struggles and sins of elders because these are proof that they can fail in various ways and still have godly outcomes.

Another source of security is that evangelists tend to come and go, but elders stay. Paul and the evangelists he sent to Crete and Ephesus eventually left, but they appointed elders who stayed with the disciples for the long haul.

Both evangelists and elders are are crucial to God's church, and they must learn to work closely together to accomplish God's purposes. This we will examine in the next chapter.

8

Leadership Relationships
Elders and Evangelists
Part Two: The "Marriage" of the Two

S

So how do the two roles of evangelist and elder—and the people in these roles—work together in the church? I believe we first must see that the roots of our modern day movement have contributed some negative baggage that can interfere with the forging of this relationship. Many of our current leaders, including the two of us writing this book, started out in ministries in which a very adversarial relationship between elders and evangelists had emerged. In traditional Churches of Christ, elders were seen as those with hiring and firing rights, while evangelists held the power of the pulpit. Instead of personal relationships, there was often a leveraging of power points to get what each wanted or felt was needed.

Many of us who were evangelists in an earlier day went through the painful process of pouring our lives into people we converted and loved for years, only to be fired by elders who disagreed with our approach to ministry. I was personally asked to leave on two different occasions.

The most frustrating part of these conflicts was that these elders were often unqualified and nonfunctional in terms of the Biblical teaching about their role. They were often wealthy or opinionated, but not spiritual. As evangelists, we were also young, idealistic and shocked by the worldly process of many such encounters. Other telling effects of the lack of spirituality were a lack of evangelism and a protection of the uncommitted by elders, rather than the elders backing those of us calling for change. Such experiences left scars and biases that later affected both our desire to become elders and our value for their role. Much like abused children who lose their trust in one or the other parent, some may have lost their trust in older disciples with the same title of "elder," but with very different hearts and mentalities.

While many of our evangelists did not grow up spiritually in such an environment, they were often trained by those who did. It is important to note that some of the attitudes that grew out of those unhealthy and sinful situations seeped down into the lives of others who were not themselves directly affected by them. Of course, those of us who serve as elders in our present movement must avoid any semblance of this past approach.

To work together we must overcome such historic memories and create new ones—based on Biblical qualifications, trust and a very different spirit that typifies our elders today. I want to address this issue because I have observed that the appointment of elders seems to be slow in coming. Many evangelists are slow to profile them and to initiate Biblical functions. They ask, "What does an elder do?"—as though it were shrouded in mystery. As a congregational elder in a large church with many regions, I formerly appointed region elders, but have since stopped. I did so after observing that unless the region evangelist was enthusiastic about the appointment and emotionally invested in the relationship, a good dynamic would not follow. In Boston, elders are now raised up and appointed only by the evangelists who will work with them.

On the positive side, we have seen more and more elders being appointed, following the inspiring examples of pioneers like Bob Gempel, Al Baird, Gordon Ferguson and their wives. These couples set lofty standards of both being elder couples and working as a team with evangelists Kip and Randy McKean in Boston and Al with Kip later in Los Angeles. Our understanding of the McKean, Baird and Gempel dynamic of team decision-making in the early Boston days has served as a guide and upward call to the McKean, Ferguson and Shaw team who now fill the roles in Boston. Kip McKean has called on every world sector leader couple to raise up elder couples around them to disciple their lives and families and to share the load of leadership responsibility.

Building a Leadership Team

I want to now share what Randy and Kay McKean, Gordon and Theresa Ferguson, and Jeanie and I have found to be most helpful in building our leadership team through the last ten years.

Friendship

Friendship has been the bedrock of building our team. We all have very different personalities, though we share some common history and/or interests. The Shaws and McKeans were converted at the University of Florida and are still Gator fans. We can often be found watching a Gator game at each others' homes, sharing the thrill of victory or the agony of defeat. Gordon and I both loved to hunt and fish while growing up in the South, and we still love to occasionally share these hobbies together. Sharing stories of trips gone by is equally fun and not as time consuming. We have spent many hours of fellowship together, sharing meals on Sunday nights, wrestling with decisions and shouldering the load together as companions and friends.

Trust

Trust has been developed through time, as we have grown in mutual respect for each others' strengths and wisdom— demonstrated in the midst of many struggles. Randy has shared his concerns about Gordon's or my convictions on critical items of discipling or ministry building. We have shared our concerns about his convictions, decisions or handling of various challenging situations or people. We have had intense debates and discussions about such matters. Each of us has been willing to be questioned, to be persuaded to change or to see we have been wrong. It has been through such time and effort that trust has been built, more by seeing one another's heart and intent, rather than by expecting perfect performance. Randy has learned to trust that we do not want to be quarterbacks and take over his role. We have learned to trust that Randy does not want to run ahead and leave us to clean up his messes. God has blessed us with an increasing measure of trust for and with one another.

Respect

Respect, like trust, must be gained through time and experience. It also must be given and asked for. I remember when we asked Randy what he thought the Biblical role of elders was. I asked if he thought they were important and essential to him and told him I did not feel like I had been treated like this was the case sometimes. He has told Gordon and me that he felt we were too negative, had listened to critics too sympathetically or did not back him up at critical junctures in meetings or in implementing decisions. We have hammered out which of these were accurate or inaccurate, facts or feelings, or a lack of respect or insecurity on any of our parts. Evangelists and elders must respect each other both when the fire is burning and when the smoke clears, but it takes honesty and wrestling to get there.

"No Fear"

"No fear" of one another's convictions, opinions or commitment to the group is another essential ingredient we have discovered in building our team. I am seeing more and more the pervasive nature of fear in disciples' relationships. Fear has to do with punishment and pain (1 John 4:18). So many dysfunctional relationships have to do with fear. Effective leadership teams remove the fear of one another's convictions and opinions. Instead, the participants learn to value others' input because it helps shape or confirm their own convictions in needed ways. I used to worry about what Randy or Gordon would think of my views, but now I welcome their perspectives when they are different from mine. I think we all feel this way now. As I said in chapter 6, we have come to believe that the decisions that come from our discussion will be right more often than not.

"No fear" of one another's commitment to the group has come to mean that there is no back door for us. In the past there were times when one or another of us was unhappy, hurt or disappointed with some aspect of our leadership group and threatened to leave by moving to perceived easier relationships and greener pastures. We discovered how this damaged the group dynamic and weakened our confidence in leading together. We could not really deal with issues for fear that some would "take their ball and go home." Eventually, we had a heart-to-heart talk in which each of us pledged to never do that again, but to work out whatever we needed to work out to be happy and content on the team. We do not believe in free agency (in the professional sports use of this term) because it produces disloyalty and the fear of a breakup. We are committed to one another and to the leadership team "till death do us part!"

Unconditional Love

I want to repeat my concern on this issue of fear, because I believe it is one of the most damaging dynamics in human relationships both within and outside of the kingdom. If you are afraid of anyone with whom you should have a close relationship, it is not healthy or godly and must be worked out. I figured out some time ago that in too many of my relationships, fear was aroused in me at points of contact or conflict. All too often, I felt and acted as a kid with a stern adult, rather than as a man to a man, or better still, as a friend to a friend. I put this realization together with 1 John 4:18, "perfect love drives out fear," and realized that I was not mature—and neither were many of my relationships. (I am forty-nine years old and just figuring some of this out!)

Many young disciples, and not a few older ones, still struggle with fear in relationships that needs to be cast out. "Perfect" love means "mature" love, and the word for love here is *agape*—the unconditional variety. "Unconditional" means, "You can't make me not love you"—which essentially means that I should not have to fear the pain or punishment of rejection or fear being "in the doghouse" or fear anger not repented of, or fear a lack of acceptance when we disagree or when I mess up. This is especially true for leaders who must daily face the pressures of making important decisions that affect thousands of people. The responsibility alone is pressure enough to tax our spiritual limits, and when it is intensified by such sinful and dysfunctional relational dynamics, even the strongest among us can shut down and/or become hurt and resentful. As I heard somewhere lately, we must put the "*fun* back in dys*fun*ctional" by at least casting out the fear!

We must feel free to share our current convictions, reservations, opinions and gut-level reactions in an atmosphere of unconditional love. Much stress is related to fear. I believe we have too much stress in leadership that directly relates to fear of one another's reactions. I remember approaching too many meetings, discussions and interactions with anticipation of fear rather than love. I no longer fear our meetings, nor do Randy, Gordon, Dan or our wives, to the best of my knowledge. We can disagree, dispute or even become emotional—without fear.

Only leaders themselves can determine to cast out fear with mature love. Jesus did not lead the disciples by means of fear, but as a friend and in love (John 15:14). We must call our people to respect leadership but not to fear it. Then and only then will our love mature and our relationships be real and honest. Casting out fear will radically change any and every group dynamic. I challenge all of us to begin with the group we are with!

Planning and Sharing the Battle

One of the greatest challenges to leadership groups is being committed to time together. I grew up in a family of ten. Suppers and Sunday lunches were times set by my parents as family gatherings only to be missed by permission. Making sure the ten of us had time together was difficult but essential for building family and for dealing with family goals, issues and growth. They solved the challenge by calling all of us to be committed to these consistent times during which we planned and shared how our lives were going in every area. You might imagine these were more than just eating times, especially if things were not good on the Wyndham front.

Such is the need for all components of our leadership group. Randy, Gordon, Dan, me and our wives all have different responsibilities and views of the battle. We must set and keep our times together as a group to guide the family and win the spiritual battle. How is your leadership dinner table?

Goals of Church-Leader Groups

> It was he who gave some to be apostles, some to be prophets, some to be evangelists, and some to be pastors and teachers, to prepare God's people for works of service, so that the body of Christ may be built up until we all reach unity in the faith and in the knowledge of the Son of God and become mature, attaining to the whole measure of the fullness of Christ. (Ephesians 4:11-13)

Paul describes the goals of church-leader groups as preparing God's people for works of service and building up the body of Christ in unity of faith, knowledge of Jesus, and Christlike maturity all around. Evangelists are to be the initiators and groundbreakers. They are the quarterbacks and should be men able to see God's vision and to clearly and forcefully advance this vision into the heart and character of the church as a whole through each disciple. They must stay the course of Biblical vision and be resolute in keeping the vision pure and applied to the character, programs and activities of the church. To utilize Barna's ideas on successful large churches again:

> The responsibilities of the [lead evangelist] are focused and limited….The [lead evangelist] is the primary change driver in the congregation.[1]

We find that by nature Randy, more than any other in our group, stays passionate about whether we are really getting God's will done evangelistically as a church and world sector. He cannot get it all done or even keep up with all that is or is not being done, but he drives the accountability and the needed changes that such evaluation reveals.

Elders are to be the "overseers," and I believe this translates into "the quality-assurance people," the part of the team that looks ahead for the unexpected or often unanticipated that has been forgotten before and likely will be again. We oversee the important that gets overlooked by evangelists who, with good intentions, do not like to take the time or attention for items that may seem less exciting but can be equally important to healthy disciples and churches.

Elders and evangelists, as leadership partners, are much like two parents who both want to raise an awesome family. Together we must figure out who is best at finances, health and hygiene issues, character development, fun (do not forget fun!), devotionals, evangelism and many other Christian family responsibilities. Elders and evangelists must divide the arenas that both know are vital but that one is more likely to overlook than the other. Together we cover one another's tendencies to forget or leave out.

Schedules, time and the speed with which life can move are enemies that team leaders must fight. The need for multitasking by top leaders is currently one of our greatest challenges as

[1]George Barna, *The Habits of Highly Effective Churches* (Ventura, Calif.: Regal Books, 1999) 28-29.

a movement, and we must continue to discover and share how to make life manageable and less stressful for leaders and leadership groups. It can be done because Jesus said, "Peace I leave with you; my peace I give you" (John 14:27).

We must keep changing in order to find both effectiveness and peace as leaders. We cannot disciple in others what we do not have ourselves. What excites me most is the humility we have had in our Boston team. I am confident that we will continue to have this humility in finding solutions.

We read this about Paul as he left the Ephesian elders: "When he had said this, he knelt down with all of them and prayed. They all wept as they embraced him and kissed him" (Acts 20:36-37). In many ways, partings are the ultimate test of what you have in relationships. Tears flowed freely when the evangelist and elders had to say good-bye. I remember leaving some places with such tears and leaving other places with more of a sense of relief. Perhaps the best test of what you now have with your team would be to imagine leaving them. Which would it be, relief or grief? Friendship, trust, respect, no fear, unconditional love, planning and sharing the battles—the stuff great leadership teams are made of—are what leads to those tears. We will all accompany one another to our ships at some time. Now is the time to determine the tears.

9

Striking the Balance

> By the grace God has given me, I laid a foundation as an
> expert builder, and someone else is building on it. But
> each one should be careful how he builds. For no one
> can lay any foundation other than the one already laid,
> which is Jesus Christ. If any man builds on this founda-
> tion using gold, silver, costly stones, wood, hay or
> straw, his work will be shown for what it is, because the
> Day will bring it to light. It will be revealed with fire, and
> the fire will test the quality of each man's work. If what
> he has built survives, he will receive his reward. If it is
> burned up, he will suffer loss; he himself will be saved,
> but only as one escaping through the flames.
>
> 1 Corinthians 3:10-15

Pouring our lives into people as we bring them to Christ is one of life's most fulfilling tasks, replete with rejoicing. Watching them fall away brings us to the other end of the emotional scale. Building wisely is one of the greatest needs set before us. If we build unwisely, according to Paul, what we build will not survive. A number of different words might be employed to describe wise building, but "balance" is one of the best.

At one time in the kingdom, some viewed the word "bal-ance" as suspect, as if its use suggested a watering down of Christ's call to total commitment. Being out of control was actu-ally advocated, and I recall the words of one excited evangelist as being something along these lines: "Get the fire of evangel-ism burning out of control and then throw gasoline on it!" Zeal for the lost should be commended, but building anything unwisely will not result in long-range, sustained growth. If we build beyond our capacity to maintain, damage will be done. Try adopting six kids at once if you think numbers are the only consideration. You will quickly develop a deeper understanding of what it means to burn out of control.

No, "balance" is not a bad word, although it could be misapplied spiritually. For example, we must learn to strike a balance in our affection and devotion to relationships. If we attempt to love God with our everything, as Matthew 22:36-40 says, without also showing love in other relationships, we could end up being so heavenly minded that we are of no earthly good. Learning to put God first, our families second, the church third, the lost next and ourselves last is all about balance. Prayerfully, this chapter will help us to build more wisely—to build with an eye to the future. We will examine several key areas in which balance must be achieved in order to ensure that our building for God will not end up being burned in the flames.

Converting People
Getting Wet Versus Conversion

The key leadership consideration in winning others to Christ is in seeing the difference between "getting baptisms" and making disciples. At one end of the spectrum is the call to win as many as possible (1 Corinthians 9:19), and at the other end is Jesus' charge to make disciples (Matthew 28:19). Surely we hardly need to mention that we can become so focused on numbers of baptisms that we neglect to make true disciples. Jesus said to make disciples, not church members. His approach in Luke 14:25-33 of counting the cost shows exactly what that difference is. We cannot "slick" people into the kingdom if they have not made a total commitment to be lifelong disciples of Jesus, knowing at least the basics of what this is going to demand of them. Counting the cost is a vital part of his message. Those who lead a double life in the kingdom introduce a spiritual cancer into the body, and they deter others who might otherwise have been open. "As it is written: 'God's name is blasphemed among the Gentiles because of you'" (Romans 2:24).

We must resist the temptation to short-cut the process of preparing someone for baptism. An overemphasis on reaching numerical goals often lies behind such temptations. For example, if the number of people who are studying the Bible in order to become disciples is low, we may back off from giving the needed challenges out of fear of having to report even lower study counts. Also, sometimes in our desire to convert opinion leaders, we become conflict avoiders and fail to push their heart buttons in order to get down to the deeper issues. As an elder, I sometimes receive calls to help with difficult situations that involve people who are successful in a worldly way, but who frankly came into the church unbroken about their sin. Mark this one down: It is much easier to help successful people become broken and humble while they are studying to become Christians than two years later when their unabated pride has grown even more. I was taught years ago that counting the cost before baptism is the time to try to talk the person out of baptism. If they can then talk you into baptizing them, this means that they are ready to become saved disciples. Although this is still my practice, which I explain up front to the person who is studying, I have the feeling that many leaders are trying so hard to talk people into baptism that they do not adequately count the cost with them.

I love seeing the truth hit the hearts of non-Christians when they realize that they are not truly saved. It is a wonderful moment. I recently heard about a man who had started studying and upon realizing his state before God, became quite urgent. As he and the man with whom he was studying were setting up their schedules for future studies, he became disturbed about schedule conflicts that kept him from studying every day. The disciple explained that they did not have to study every day and could work around his schedule. The man's reply was classic: "Easy for you to say—you're already saved." Wow! He really got the point!

However, as important as developing urgency is, it must be the non-Christian's urgency driving him and not our urgency. Some months back, I baptized a man who had previously been "pushed" into baptism before his heart was ready. From the moment of baptism, he knew that he did not truly become a Christian. Although he continued to attend services, mainly to please his wife, he resisted all attempts at converting him. In looking back on his study experiences, he felt like a "number" more than like a person—that he was merely important for meeting a goal. Of course, we can argue that his fear of being manipulated was more imagined than real, but he did not imagine *everything* he felt. Once I built enough of a relationship with him, he opened up to the gospel in a wonderful way and is now an exemplary disciple of Jesus.

Our job in studying the Bible with people is to bring them to the point of having a spiritual encounter with the Christ. It is God who must create urgency in their hearts and ultimately bring them into his kingdom. The studies are never about us and them; they are all about God and them. Paul clarified this principle:

> I planted the seed, Apollos watered it, but God made it grow.
> So neither he who plants nor he who waters is anything, but
> only God, who makes things grow. (1 Corinthians 3:6-7)

We cannot force anyone to repent; we cannot "break" anyone. We can only volunteer to be vessels for God to use, and as such, we do all that we can and pray that "God will grant them repentance leading them to a knowledge of the truth" (2 Timothy 2:25).

I love studying with honest people who are not afraid to say what is on their minds. Rather than feeling intimidated by their outspokenness or frustrated that they are not quickly acquiescing to what I am teaching, I rejoice that we are dealing with the real issues. They may say something along these lines (with a bit of an attitude): "Does that mean that I'm lost? Do you really think I'm lost?" My replies go something like this: "Well, what I think about the matter is not the issue; nor is what you think so important. What matters is what God thinks, and I know what he thinks because he wrote it in the Book. Now please read that passage again, and tell me what God says about your spiritual condition right now."

We must learn how to lead all types of people and then to train other leaders to do the same. Building wisely means that we deal with the heart until it is ready, and this usually means that we must hit some serious "bumps" with those studying and help them get past them. Dodging the issues may get someone into the baptistry quicker, but it may not get them into Christ at all. Be careful; build wisely.

A young woman who is a family group leader told me recently about an interaction she had with her ministry leader about reaching such goals. Feeling that she was being pushed to "get the baptism" by the end of the month, she found the courage to be honest. The conversation went something like this:

> "Can you get the woman baptized by the end of the week?"
>
> "I really doubt it, given where she is at this point."
>
> "Well, if you had more faith, you could."
>
> "The issue here is not my faith; it's the faith of the woman in the study."
>
> "But if you really pushed her hard, she could make it."
>
> "We are the ones who have to live with her after she's baptized, and I'm not willing to push her beyond where her faith is."
>
> End of conversation.

We need more people with enough common sense to speak up about building wisely. Just do it—respectfully.

Personally, I am deeply disturbed about ministry groups who baptize large numbers in a push month, only to see many of these people fall away a few months later. In the realm of eating, the binge and purge syndrome has a name, and it is not a sign of health. Would you rather have one hundred baptisms in a year with eighty of these who fall away, resulting in a net growth of twenty people in your ministry; or thirty baptisms with ten who fall away, also resulting in a net growth of twenty people? (Sure, sure, I would rather have one hundred baptisms with only ten who fall away too, but please answer the question.) When large numbers of people leave, there are at least three highly disconcerting results. One, it is a tragedy in the life of the one who leaves—whose heart, at one time, had presumably been contrite about sin and devoted to God and the family of believers—and it has devastating consequences for their souls. Two, some of the most fervent persecutors of the kingdom come from those who have left us. The bigger the pool, the higher the number of potential persecutors. (How many potential converts do you know who have been poisoned by disgruntled people who have left?) Three, the faith of those who originally studied the Bible with a person who later falls away is hit—and hit hard.

I remember one family group leader telling me about baptizing eight people in a few months, only to have six of them fall away quickly, with the other two barely hanging on. He openly admitted his own faith struggle and that of his people when it came to being fired up about another evangelistic push. Consistent growth from people who have been converted the right way is required for long-range, healthy progress in the church.

Weak Versus Strong Character

We must also strike a balance in the types of people we convert. Interestingly, most of our mistakes in this area also come from taking shortcuts to grow numerically. As a result, we end up working with people who can more easily be persuaded to study, but who may not have the character to contribute significantly to the ongoing process of evangelism. It seems to me that a common mistake is to have ministry staff jump in on Bible studies in order to baptize quickly, which leads to two basic weaknesses in building: (1) those not on staff are not allowed to conduct their own studies and (2) staff members do not focus enough on reaching those with more leadership potential. Paul told Timothy to entrust what he had learned to "reliable men" who would also be "qualified to teach others" (2 Timothy 2:2). It should be obvious that converting a majority of people who could be described as *unreliable* in character will not build a foundation that sustains growth in the long run. *This is not to say that any person is unimportant or does not need to be saved*; but it is to say that building without regard for balance will likely result in them being unsaved anyway. Unless sufficient numbers of people with leadership potential are converted and raised up, those with weaker character cannot be cared for properly, and many will fall away.

In my book *Revolution!* I noted that the conversion of opinion leaders was a recurring theme. What I wrote there is worth repeating here:

> Philip was sent by God to convert an opinion leader, the treasurer of an entire nation. This is the first of many such instances in the book of Acts, and the accounts are included for a highly significant reason: Opinion leaders are usually more difficult to convert (obviously not always), but without such conversions, the mission will ultimately fail. These people have a following with whom they have great influence, and they can soon be fruitful—abundantly fruitful. Just as importantly, they can rise up quickly to become leaders. If you want to build a ministry that is sure to fail, convert only nonopinion leaders. I have seen denominational churches do it time and time again. It is not the plan of God, as may be seen in this and

numerous accounts. According to tradition, this eunuch went back to his home country and built quite a church.[1]

The conversion of Sergius Paulus, the proconsul in the city of Paphos on the island of Crete, is yet another example of the conversion of a prominent opinion leader (Acts 13:6-12). The numerous similar accounts in Acts can be viewed as nothing less than a divinely sanctioned pattern for church plantings. Both Biblically and practically, the first people converted in new locations will become the first leaders there. And if those with leadership abilities are not among the first converted, then the planting is certain to struggle and falter. Establishing churches by converting a strong base of leaders is the way of God, and nothing less will suffice to get the job done. A classic example of the pattern is seen in 1 Corinthians 16:15-16:

> You know that the household of Stephanas were the first converts in Achaia, and they have devoted themselves to the service of the saints. I urge you, brothers, to submit to such as these and to everyone who joins in the work, and labors at it.

The first converts in Corinth became the heart of the church. Whether Sergius Paulus became *the* leader of the church in Paphos we cannot know for certain; but that he became *a* leader there seems highly probable.

Make no mistake about it: Long-range growth depends largely on having a pool of leaders available to help disciple and lead newer converts. The work of those like Scott and Lynne Green in Hong Kong provides an outstanding modern day example of such wise and effective building. Their focus on converting those with strong leadership potential enabled them to raise up many young leaders quickly. The more needy the converts are emotionally, the greater the need to have many quality leaders raising up to meet those needs. This situation is a bit tricky.

[1]Gordon Ferguson, *Revolution! The World-Changing Church in the Book of Acts* (Billerica, Mass.: Discipleship Publications International, 1998) 84.

When congregations are newer and smaller, even those with weaker character do better, primarily because they have more fellowship and relationship with the ministry staff. They feel like they are "in" the "inner group." As churches grow, more levels of leadership develop, and the weak do not do nearly as well. You can end up with the weak discipling the weaker, making spiritual growth difficult to achieve.

I heard one good suggestion recently for addressing this particular need. It is to have a discipleship group of weaker disciples led by a mature leader who has a proven record of helping the weak. Instead of arranging discipleship partners within this group, disciples are simply paired off with one another as prayer partners. The discipleship group provides the right teaching and discipling diet, and having a spiritual buddy takes care of other relational needs. This approach eliminates the over/under structure that is more easily abused among younger and weaker disciples anyway.

In the marrieds ministry, a grow-at-all-costs approach causes us to go after those who are easier to reach (weaker character). After conversion, their serious marriage and family problems require a disproportionate amount of time from stronger disciples. Those with weaker character can be baptized more quickly, but should not be. If they come into the kingdom with a low success rate in overcoming their weaknesses, they will quickly become discouraged and fall away. If they experience success in making significant changes before baptism, then they tend to be more faithful about continuing to change. Converting wives without pulling out all of the stops to reach their husbands, even to the point of slowing down the studies of the wives, will destroy balance and lead to an unhealthy ministry. Yes, I know that these spiritually minded women need to be converted, but I also know that if you handle the situation unwisely, they could end up in the divorce court.

Perhaps you are feeling a bit of tension as you read this section, wondering if I am suggesting showing favoritism or preferential treatment of persons. In view of what James 2:1-5 says, I certainly don't intend to move anyone in that direction. It is not an issue of one person being more valuable than another at all; it is an issue of building in a manner that sustains growth. I think that some show partiality in another way. If we are motivated to baptize for worldly reasons (to reach our goals so that we can feel "successful"), we can focus on those who are easiest to reach and then later find ourselves resenting their weaknesses and the amount of time it takes to work with them. This constitutes conditional love, if it can be defined as love at all. Giving a potential candidate for baptism lavish attention before baptism, only to pull back from him or her later on when deeper character sins start coming out, leaves people feeling very unloved and unappreciated.

We need the weak, according to 1 Corinthians 12:21-25.

> The eye cannot say to the hand, "I don't need you!" And the head cannot say to the feet, "I don't need you!" On the contrary, those parts of the body that seem to be weaker are indispensable, and the parts that we think are less honorable we treat with special honor. And the parts that are unpresentable are treated with special modesty, while our presentable parts need no special treatment. But God has combined the members of the body and has given greater honor to the parts that lacked it, so that there should be no division in the body, but that its parts should have equal concern for each other.

Our goal must be to make the weak strong—in terms of Hebrews 11:34, to turn weaknesses to strengths. If we really disciple people well after conversion, newer disciples should not remain weak on a long-term basis. However, in the real world, those coming into the kingdom with weak character are not going to change as quickly nor as easily as those whose backgrounds were more healthy. We need the weak and we must love the weak, but converting too many with substantially weak character will result in promising what we are not equipped to deliver. As we go about our mission, enough leaders must be converted to help care for all of the rest. It is a question of common sense.

Converting too many foreigners is also counterproductive. Converting too many minorities in areas where they are not strongly represented in that societal setting is likewise fraught with problems. (A nearly all-white or all-black church group should send up some red flags, unless the societal setting is of that nature.) Converting more single women than men will wreak havoc as well, especially if the women tend to have more leadership qualities than the men, as is often true. Women without consistent dates and with the perception that their marriage potential may be quite limited face serious temptations to compromise their convictions—thus leading to many who fall away. My suggestion would be to strongly consider having the whole church concentrate on converting single men for as long as it takes to offset this unbalanced situation. This means that marrieds should concentrate on this as well as the single sisters. Obviously, training is needed to know how to go about this.

Some of our churches that have made mistakes in building poorly have now lost so much faith that they have an aversion to setting goals or taking numerical growth seriously. Please, let's avoid compounding the problem with this mistake. We should grow; we can grow; we must grow. The need of the hour is to make sure that we are doing it by building wisely. One helpful suggestion is to focus accountability on *process* rather than simply on the bottom line of *numbers* baptized. For example, if we helped disciples concentrate on building strong relationships with non-Christians, we would baptize and more likely build wisely at the same time. When morale and faith have been lost as a result of poor building, we must do all that it takes to get back our zeal to multiply true disciples. And yet this is certain: how we convert people and who we convert are worthy topics for discussion among leaders. Strike the balance.

Motivating Potential Leaders

The Ambition to Lead

Constantly raising up and training all types of new leaders is an important part of building the kingdom; hence, we must make leadership a goal to be desired and sought after. A large percentage of our people can certainly grow into leading Bible talks. This should be seen as a worthy goal for which most should strive. We also need leaders who can carry even more responsibility, including those on the ministry staff supported by the church. However, motivating people who seek to become part of the ministry staff is tricky. If we are not careful, we set up expectations for people that are not realistic in light of their leadership gifts. In this case, if they cannot reach this goal, they are left with very negative feelings about themselves and their futures. We have many in our fellowship who have these feelings, if they are willing to be honest about it. One way to avoid this dilemma is suggested in my book *The Power of Spiritual Thinking*:

> One danger is that we can become far too focused on positional goals in the church and become unspiritual in the process. Some have set their hearts on leadership positions that are frankly beyond the scope of their spiritual gifts. They are set up for disappointment and disillusionment in God, themselves and the kingdom. Those who set their hearts on goals that they do not and cannot reach will feel like failures and second-class citizens. I am far more comfortable with living by what I call the "Joseph principle."[2]

Joseph had no idea that he could be the second-in-command of the greatest nation on earth (Genesis 41:37-43). He

[2]Gordon Ferguson, *The Power of Spiritual Thinking* (Billerica, Mass.: Discipleship Publications International, 2000) 61-62.

was a slave and a prisoner for thirteen years. The only ambition that seemed possible for him was that of serving and trusting God to the best of his ability on a daily basis. But because that was his heart, God was able to exalt him beyond his wildest imagination. What if each of us lived each day with one thought in mind—to be as much like Jesus as possible? Do you really think that the church would be short on leaders?

The Gift to Lead

We need to be honest about the nature of and differences in our gifts, as described in Romans 12:3-8. Leadership is a gift of God, as are the other gifts that are mentioned. Gifts are just that—gifts. We do not earn them nor deserve them, nor are we superior because we have them. If we rely on them in a prideful manner, gifts become obstacles to our own growth and to seeing our need for others. For example, I have a reasonably good intellect (although my mind's computer is definitely slowing down with age!). Why? From a divine perspective, it is because of God's gifts. But from a human perspective, it is principally because of my gene pool. I could just as easily have been born with a low IQ or with significant learning disabilities. The fact that I have good learning capabilities has nothing to do with my value at all. If 1 Corinthians 12 teaches anything, it is that in the family of God, no one is inferior and no one is superior.

Truthfully, we are more humanistic than we may think. We value some gifts more than others, but I do not think God does. For example, my best gifts are more the up-front variety. I am a teacher and preacher with the gift of gab, and I write pretty well also. I often receive attention and praise for those gifts. I always remind myself that the Corinthian church had more spiritual gifts than about any other church, and yet they were the most unspiritual of the lot. Having gifts does not mean that we are spiritual; it only means that we have been blessed of God with gifts that are intended to bring him glory, not us. Properly understood, our gifts ought to humble us, not puff us up.

My wife, Theresa, is a gifted person. In terms of Romans 12, she has a number of gifts that are much more developed than my qualities in the same categories, specifically these: serving, encouraging, giving and showing mercy. These gifts are more the behind-the-scenes types of gifts, while my best gifts are not. What are often the results of these differences in our two sets of gifts? I receive most of the notice, and she often feels less important than me to the church and even to God (just being honest, and yes, we are working on viewing these things spiritually). Why? Because we tend to value the types of gifts that the world values—the more visible leadership gifts. Which types do you think God treasures most in us? Easy answer—the types that are most connected to character and heart. On Judgment Day, I would rather meet God with my beloved wife's gifts than with my own, without question. We need to develop God's viewpoint on these things:

> But the LORD said to Samuel, "Do not consider his appearance or his height, for I have rejected him. The LORD does not look at the things man looks at. Man looks at the outward appearance, but the LORD looks at the heart." (1 Samuel 16:7)

All in all, we must raise up leaders of all types, but we are going to have to work carefully to avoid making people feel inferior when their gifts do not match with certain roles. Different gifts and different roles we have; different values to God and to one another, we do not have. As leaders, we simply must learn how to get this message across in a sensitive way. It may be easy to ascertain how effective we are in motivating people to want to be a part of the ministry staff, but it is very difficult to measure the long-term negative effects of motivating in the wrong way. In our physical families, we hopefully are very careful about making every child feel special and never inferior. In God's family, we cannot afford to do less. Golden Rule leadership demands it.

Feeding the Flock

Sustaining growth is a matter of feeding the sheep a balanced diet. In chapter 12 we will discuss the need for building a deeper Biblical knowledge into our ministry staff and entire membership. I have already noted the need for our teaching to have more of a God-focus and less of a man-focus. Suffice it to say that our teaching needs to have balance in both content and delivery.

The grace/works balance is one of the most fundamental to maintain. We tend to be very heavy on the works side of the ledger. I remember an older preacher in my former church who honestly thought it was a mistake to preach on grace because it might encourage people to let down their efforts. He thought it more effective to keep them feeling as if their feet were dangling over the fires of hell, for then they would stay really motivated. If we adopt the philosophy that the Golden Rule of leadership is to treat God's children like you want your own to be treated, then we can reject my former associate's viewpoint outright. No child, physical or spiritual, can thrive under such a load.

We are prone to focus on man's responsibilities more than on God's grace. Why? One thought is that our preachers are males, and males like the short version of things. My wife and I talk about the male version and the female version, and at times I ask her to give me the male version instead of the female! Cut to the chase and get to the bottom line—this is the way of most of us males. For example, when we preach from Ephesians or Colossians, where do we typically begin? We begin in mostly the chapters of application rather than in the principles in the first chapters which provide the foundation for those applications in the first place. God's teaching was designed to remove burdens, not add them. "This is love for God: to obey his commands. And his commands are not burdensome" (1 John 5:3). Look up the word "burden" in the New Testament, and you will find that the writers were especially interested in not being a burden to the people. God's commands are not burdensome, if (and this is a big *if*) you preach enough grace for them to fall in love and stay in love with the Commandment-Giver!

A related area of striking a balance in teaching and preaching is between critique and encouragement. Someone has said that we need at least ten "encouragements" to be able to accept one critique. I think it may be higher than that; it is certainly not lower for most of us. We have lived most of our lives feeling put down, and this feeling is not dispelled quickly or easily. Of the sixty-two mentions in the New Testament of our "one another" and "each other" responsibilities, they are overwhelmingly positive. We are either told to treat one another with grace or to stop doing otherwise. Only two of these occurrences suggest corrective relationship dynamics: Colossians 3:16 speaks of admonishing one another, and Hebrews 10:24 speaks of the need to "spur one another on toward love and good deeds." That is it, Biblically, but is that it in your teaching, preaching and discipling? *The idea that leaders are mainly those who find faults in others and fix them is a really bad idea.* It does not promote spiritual health, being much more likely to promote spiritual insecurity and paranoia.

My judgment is that the majority of us tend toward being out of balance on the side of works and critique. However, being out of balance on the other side of the coin is just as wrong. We are sinners and we need to be challenged. People do not need to be entertained—they need a message from God, and it needs to have the appropriate challenges in it. It is fine to display some qualities of a comedian or a dramatic actor in the pulpit, but this is not what correctly handling the word of truth (2 Timothy 2:15) is all about. People may be of the MTV generation, but this is not the diet they need, even with a spiritual twist on it. We become overly concerned about how our audience will respond to straight teaching. I do not intend to compete with glitzy entertainment. In fact, watching some of the popular talk shows on television convinces me that "there is no fear of God before their eyes" (Romans 3:18).

The Holy Spirit was sent into the world by Jesus to "convict the world of guilt in regard to sin and righteousness and judgment" (John 16:8). You are a tool of God through whom the Holy Spirit must work. Do not soften his message nor eliminate any part of it as you serve. But do not get out of balance on either side. "Consider therefore the kindness and sternness of God" (Romans 11:22). We need both to stay in balance.

Other areas of balance in a Biblically healthy diet could be mentioned, but these are some of the key ones. Let's go to work on these, and God will show us the other areas. Just please treat God's children like you want your own to be treated. It is the Golden Rule of ministry.

10

Small Groups and Golden Rule Practice

Recently there has been much emphasis on the return to small groups in discipling ministry. I believe we are seeing that this is the fundamental building block of body life and ministry. While emphasis on worship attendance does not have to pre-empt small group development, it seems we have a hard time focusing on two things at once—like walking and chewing gum, as my old friend Tom Brown used to say. Once we began to put the emphasis on our Sunday assemblies, many of us began to put less focus on small groups. However, Jesus himself used small groups with his disciples to build individual and group maturity that reproduces itself. New Testament references to house churches, "two or three" gathering in Jesus' name, and bands of brothers sent out who centered around apostles like Paul, all point to the power of small groups. They were used for training, working, worshiping and growing together.

In this book we are focused on building or rebuilding groups at all levels where people are treated according to the Golden Rule. In small groups, disciples have the greatest opportunity to learn to treat each other in this way, thus becoming attractive beacons to non-Christians and healthy microcosms of growth for all disciples. Much has already been said about building groups at the leadership level. I want to focus in this chapter on building them at the grass-roots level. The greatest challenge in building ministries is usually not figuring out good and Biblically sound theory; it's keeping it applied to each disciple as the ministry gets larger and older.

Impact Replication

Managing needs, discipling people and growing the church numerically and spiritually become very difficult if one leader tries to keep up with it all and have it revolve around him. Breaking down into small groups facilitates assessment, specific teaching and prayer, allowing leaders to better manage the growth process for all. It also allows leaders to reduce stress and raise up others who can lead. Church leaders can teach small group leaders to replicate their efforts and therefore spread their impact in ways they could never have done if they were working alone. This was the simple but profound message of Moses' father-in-law that produced satisfaction for the people of Israel, kept Jethro's daughter married to her husband (ever wonder how he heard about the problems?) and let Moses get a life beyond counseling people with problems twenty-four/seven. Most of us in ministry leadership can relate to Moses before Exodus 18, but the real question is whether we have found the freedom and refreshment that came after the talk about organizing God's people in groups.

Of course just placing disciples' names in group arrangements on paper will not produce healthy, faithful and fruitful microcosms of the church. The theory of small-group ministry must be taught, caught and practiced by everyone in the group. Each disciple must be a willing partner for his or her spiritual team, emotionally committed to participate in loving, encouraging, working, praying and growing in the Lord. Every team member must understand and be committed to growing the group in terms of the qualities of discipleship and body life spelled out in the Scriptures. Spiritual families will attract the lost by their faith, love, joy and abundant lifestyle. Evangelism will truly be telling the good news of what they have found and a demonstration of Jesus' impact on people in the group.

I can recall groups that I have been a part of that modeled Bible teaching with willing and faithful hearts. I remember starting as a new disciple with a Bible talk in Jennings Hall at the University of Florida in my junior year. Tom Brown led it and several of us worked together as a team. By year's end, five guys from my floor had been baptized, including Sheridan Wright and Paul Ramsey, both leaders in large churches today. I remember my first small group studies at North Carolina State. Back then, I led five groups per week the first semester until my wife joined me in December and others could be raised up. Starting with a group of five or six students and a few singles and marrieds, we saw 102 baptisms in twelve months. We went from five groups of two or three Christians each to ten groups of ten or more Christians in one school year. Farm House Fraternity began as a small group of two, and in two years we had baptized ten young men into Christ. As I have grown older and led marrieds ministries here in Boston, I have been a part of small groups that have mirrored this kind of growth. Working together with Tom and Sheila Jones in one such group, we saw five or six baptisms take place in less than a year. Since then, the Fredericks, Shaws and Drakes have had groups that have baptized six to eight disciples in a year's time. Such faith-building experiences have always been highlights of my Christian life. These groups were characterized by good feelings of love, faith, fun and family, lived out by all who shared the group life together.

On the other hand, all of us have experienced groups that have been far less fruitful and have even occasioned painful experiences of disunity, complacency and faithlessness. Satan will always seek to use these very sins to destroy God's power within a ministry group. Golden Rule leadership must not hesitate to confront sin in the group. All of us enjoy leading when everyone is growing and doing well spiritually; the real test of leadership is when discipline and challenge are needed to restore lost spirituality. We must keep a clear vision of what a healthy group looks like in order to identify what to go after when one or more disciples become trapped by Satan. This is why good examples of growing groups must be held up as flesh and blood reference points for others.

Training 101

One of the most important tasks of the ministry staff is to raise up, inspire and train nonstaff small-group leaders. I believe that this task is crucial for several key reasons. First, the small group leaders are the main connection of staff to the grass roots of a church. Failure to stay closely in touch with them and their relationship dynamics within their groups is the first stage in the development of a clergy-laity mentality. The way the staff is perceived throughout the church will mainly be shaped by the small group leaders.

A second key reason that training small-group leaders is so crucial is they are the first response team to any need in a group. If as leaders they do not correctly identify personal needs, sin problems and open doors in the lives of disciples in their group, there will be undealt-with sin, missed opportunities evangelistically and unmet needs that lead to unhealthy and unhappy disciples in that group. I believe that with the recent de-emphasis on small groups, the training in how to meet the group's needs has greatly suffered. As a necessary Golden Rule training tool, leaders' meetings must be conducted with a consciousness of the time constraints of group leaders, yet they must be sufficiently long to adequately equip the leaders.

A third reason leadership training is so crucial for small-group leaders is that most who occupy this role do not have good role models for loving, building family or leading spiritually. Our tendency is to select leaders for their zeal, evangelistic success and worldly talent. None of these necessarily makes for good Golden Rule leadership. Many highly motivated disciples who are successful in their jobs are products of performance-driven parents who knew how to achieve. Loving, nurturing and encouraging diverse groups of people may prove very challenging to someone who has never seen it modeled in his own life. A family group of disciples can represent one of the most wide-ranging groups of humanity on earth. Such diversity should be viewed as good, but it does not make it easy to disciple or develop spiritual maturity, person by person. This takes training and tests the skill and maturity of the best of those on our ministry staff.

Meeting the Need

Dean and Kim Farmer, who lead the church in Berlin, offered the best advice I have ever heard for successful small-group leader training when they recently explained how they conduct their Bible talk leader meetings. Most of their time and focus is not spent on a lesson, but on building small victories that lead to larger victories, on a group by group basis. If you are a staff member who doesn't get to preach in a public forum, you will be tempted to use the Bible talk leader setting as an opportunity to preach, and to preach too long. Fight the temptation and train your people instead. For instance, if a group is not united, Dean and Kim don't focus on bringing visitors, but on dealing with sinful attitudes and disunity issues until the victory of unity is achieved—to the glory of God. They help a leader deal with such needs until unity can be rejoiced in by all. If a group is united but not having success at outreach, they talk over ideas that will help that leader again come up with small victories—such as having non-Christians into their homes or initiating in fun activities with them. They trust that God and the building process will lead that group to get people to church or find studies that will then lead to baptisms.

Also, if a group has baptized people but has seen disciples fall away regularly, they will recognize that this is an unhealthy situation. They will examine the leader's skill in nurturing and meeting disciples' needs. They might discover that the leader knows how to motivate people but not how to love and develop their faith. The focus for that leader might be very different from the first two examples mentioned.

I believe that a huge mistake made by many staff members at Bible talk or family group leader meetings is to treat all leaders as though they and their group are at the same place, have the same skills, or need the same message any given week. Golden Rule leaders take people where they are and fit the discipling to individual needs. Such training demands that spiritual health is the focus of leadership for every group leader and group. The question asked is always how to "supply what is lacking in your faith" (1 Thessalonians 3:10), whether in the leader or in the group. The reigning conviction is that spiritual health will lead to lasting growth. However, we must take the time and effort to produce growth one victory at a time.

At the heart of Golden Rule leadership is the conviction that every group of disciples is "full of goodness, complete in knowledge and competent to instruct one another" (Romans 15:14). We also hold that every disciple deserves to be treated as we would treat our own children, in terms of love, perseverance and heartfelt honesty.

Small groups allow the leadership in a church to know that every disciple is in a position to enjoy a place of belonging, family and spiritual nurturing. The groups help ensure that everyone is in a place where needs can be met and where they can contribute to saving other souls. It is through the training of small group leaders, however, that each small-group team is actually going to develop the qualities of real spirituality and abundant living. Public worship services, or even great preaching, will not give us the quality control needed for real spirituality and abundant living.

Most of us were drawn to the kingdom by experiencing the love of disciples on a personal basis. Most of us will remain disciples only as the same process continues throughout our years in the kingdom—until we go to heaven where there will be no tears, pain or death. Small groups must be our little piece of heaven on earth. Golden Rule leaders know how much their group of closest Christians means to them and will be determined to do to others as has been done for them!

11

The Pursuit of Unity

Keeping a group working together for a significant period of time is a common goal shared by parents, teachers, coaches, generals, presidents and church leaders. Forging common goals, convictions, effort and spirit, and maintaining them through time with a growing number of people, is one of the greatest tests of leadership. Failures to sustain unity are easier to find than successes.

The Historical Challenge of Unity

Examples of disunity abound as groups grow in size and age. From the rise and fall of ancient empires, such as Egyptian, Hebrew, Persian, Greek and Roman, to the breakup of the more recent British, French and Spanish Empires, we see the challenge of building and sustaining worldwide unity. The American Civil War was primarily a war to maintain a united group of states.

The fall of the Soviet Union has led to the struggle for unity in a new Commonwealth of Independent States. The present attempt to build the European Union with a common currency and language of commerce recognizes the value of unity. The challenge of uniting people with diverse cultures, languages and histories into a cohesive, functioning group is daunting. Closer to home, the growing divorce rate and breakup of more than fifty percent of our homes illustrates the challenge of just keeping small family groups united.

Biblical examples also illustrate the challenge of producing and keeping unity among God's people. King David could not keep his own family united, as seen by the painful treason of his own son Absalom (2 Samuel 15). The chosen tribes of Israel soon divided into northern and southern kingdoms, as God's leaders failed to keep his people and cause united.

In the New Testament the struggle of uniting the diverse characters chosen to be apostles and the cultural and religious backgrounds of Jew and Gentile taxed leaders and tested God's patience again and again. Peter, Paul, James and John wrestled with leadership roles, responsibilities and personal example, according to Galatians 1 and 2, to keep Jewish and Gentile Christians united. The apostles, elders and body of Christians in Jerusalem spent time in discussion, prayer and decision-making over what convictions would be required of every disciple versus what would be left up to each individual (Acts 15). False apostles and leaders who sought to make themselves first, like Diotrephes (3 John 9), along with false teachers and fallen away disciples, like Demas (2 Timothy 4:10), challenged the unity of the early church. Even tensions between proven men and women leaders like Paul and Barnabas (Acts 15:36-41) and the women of Philippi (Philippians 4:2-3) illustrate the challenge of unity in Biblical times.

The Present Challenge of Unity

My personal experience in our present religious world has been that unity continues be a great challenge for all who would know and practice God's will. Growing up, I heard the plea of denominational (divided) churches to ignore the huge differences in doctrine and unite in our common love for Jesus. The issues to be ignored included such matters as whether the Bible is inspired, whether Jesus really rose from the dead, how people become Christians and whether they need to be born again, the purpose of baptism, and whether one needs to be involved with an organized group of Christians (the church). I realized that while the Reformation Movement had rightly reacted to the non-Biblical system of

Catholicism, it had not produced a Biblical unity in its place. It was revealing and refreshing to me at age nineteen to be exposed to the concept of restoring New Testament Christianity and to use the Bible as the single standard for defining truth for all. The Restoration Movement, as I came to understand it, at least philosophically, provided a means to produce united churches of Christ held together by hearts committed to practicing what the Bible taught.

My idealism was soon shattered. While the idea of restoring Biblical Christianity was professed, the commitment to build and maintain such standards in individual lives and church groups was sadly lacking. Leaders tolerated a lack of unity both within and among individual churches in the name of not losing members and of local church autonomy. Conflicts and sin between individuals and between leaders were allowed to go unreconciled and were minimized as personality conflicts. Churches not only rarely held any kind of united services or ministry efforts, but leaders deliberately criticized those who tried to—and justified their own lack of effort in the name of autonomy. The result was frustration and a loss of faith and idealism to many young converts and leaders like me. I could not justify Jesus' and Paul's teachings and the New Testament example of kingdom and brotherhood unity with the practices around me.

The challenge of how to build and maintain unity among Christians at a local and worldwide level is not insurmountable—or God would not have commanded it. I am happy to say that God allowed me to journey on through much pain and conflict to a doctrinally and practically united place where, for the last twenty years, I have enjoyed a unified local and worldwide brotherhood among the International Churches of Christ. This unity and brotherhood has not been easily built or maintained, but it is refreshingly closer to the Biblical ideal and has weathered initial, though admittedly short-lived, success. My goal in this chapter is to share what God has taught me about what it takes for leaders and followers in God's churches to experience the unity God desires for us and for his glory.

The Value of Unity

Many spiritual groups have failed to build and maintain unity as God desires it because they fail to value it as God does. Leaders have failed to make every effort to maintain the unity of the Spirit and therefore have lost the right to speak on his behalf. The Bible speaks plainly and decisively about the value of unity and its priority for spiritual leadership:

> The LORD said, "If as one people speaking the same language they have begun to do this, then nothing they plan to do will be impossible for them." (Genesis 11:6)

Unity is a fundamental ingredient to success in any human endeavor. With it, all things are said to be possible. Without it, the converse is also true. God chose to divide this group of people in Genesis because they were united in a selfish cause. He will continue to do so with any group that is ultimately opposed to his purpose. The power of unity is illustrated by God even in this negative example.

Unity must be understood by every leader as that which is irreplaceable in a movement, church, small group within a church, and in families if each is to be successful in its mission and goals. In John 17:20-23 Jesus' priority in prayer before he died was for the unity of not only his disciples or apostles but also "for those who will believe in me through their message." This means that every group of true disciples who have lived since he spoke these words are meant to be completely united. Jesus states the crucial reason why unity must be so valued by all disciples in verse 23: "to let the world know that you sent me and have loved them even as you have loved me." Unity of believers is one of the most vital keys to evangelism, according to Jesus. No amount of boldness in sharing our faith can substitute for the evangelistic impact of a spiritually united fellowship of disciples who are truly one in heart and mind. I will never forget the impact this kind of love and unity had on me when I first experienced it in the campus ministry in Gainesville, Florida.

Unless we come to value unity as leaders and disciples, we will not make every effort to maintain it—or continue to be blessed by God. It is easier for some of us to lose conviction about unity's connection to God's blessing sooner than baptism's connection to it. The traditional Churches of Christ certainly did so. We must learn the lesson they failed to learn or else repeat the mistake others have made at the price of God's blessing and our own pain.

The Enemies of Unity

To produce and preserve unity, we must understand its enemies, whether found in others or ourselves. The Bible speaks to specific obstacles of godly unity.

Selfish Human Ambition

One of the first examples of an enemy of unity is in Genesis 11—selfish human ambition. God did not scatter these early men and women because unity was bad, but because their motives were bad. They wanted to build something contrary to God's will, centered on selfish gain. Leadership often hangs between the motives of "for God" or "for me." Parents may raise children to extend their own dreams and ambitions, coaches may coach for their own egos, politicians may run for office to advance their personal agendas, and church leaders and small-group leaders or new disciples may lead or follow for what they get out of it, versus for the glory of God. Ask yourself the question: Why do I do what I do as a disciple? Only if the question can genuinely be answered, "to bring glory to God and unity to God's people" have you defeated the number one enemy of unity building in your group.

Competition

A second enemy of unity is found in 3 John 9 in which Diotrephes is singled out for destroying unity because of loving to be first. This spiritual disease that attacks unity would be called "competition" today. John cites it as having two deadly effects on unity. It first leads to malicious gossip or verbal attacks on other leaders and then to isolation and separation within the fellowship. Competition always leads to comparisons that seek to rank self ahead of others, rather than appreciating their strengths and shared loads. I am personally not unfamiliar with the competitive nature, as those who know me can attest. But I do seek to avoid using comparative language such as "best," "biggest" or "most spiritual." As my wife says, "There is a fine line between wanting to be *our* best and wanting to be *the* best." The first usually comes from humility and the second usually comes from pride. I believe that when we describe ourselves, our ministries or ministers with such language, we move dangerously close to loving to be first and becoming competitors with our brothers, rather than companions.

All the *Diotrepheses* are not dead. How much is he alive in you or me? I like to hear Randy talk about Gordon and me as his favorite elders in the kingdom and would hope he is happy with us and not wishing for some others. Likewise, I often speak of Randy as my favorite world sector leader, and I think such subjective attachment is appropriate and healthy. But I do not believe that there is a best and worst elder or world sector leader in the kingdom, and I think when we allow ourselves to make comparisons with ourselves and to ourselves, Diotrephes is not far from our hearts. Gossip can follow quickly. Then a separation or isolation from brothers with whom we need to stay united can follow, first in our hearts and then in our fellowship.

Jumping to Conclusions

A third passage in which several enemies of unity can be identified is Joshua 22. We find the story of Joshua sending the two and a half tribes back to the other side of the Jordan River after the conquest of Canaan. With good intentions, these tribes constructed a replica of God's altar that led to near disaster. What happened when these brothers began living on the other side of the river is very revealing about enemies of unity. The first enemy that emerges is that of jumping to conclusions about our brothers' motives. The leaders of the ten tribes assumed that the brothers across the river were in deep sin, they jumped to a wrong conclusion.

I recently felt some distance between me and my good friend Al Baird. This came as a result of some intense phone talks we had had over several different issues that had come up over a year's time. I had sent Al an e-mail expressing what I thought was a fairly vulnerable appeal for reassurance about our friendship. When I did not hear back from him, I started jumping to conclusions about how Al felt about me and whether he still valued my friendship and other such thoughts. A needed conversation at a joint meeting we attended cleared everything up and revealed that Al had never felt any different after the conversations and had just assumed all was well. I jumped to a wrong conclusion that resulted in unnecessary anxiety and bad feelings on my part.

Time, Distance and Size

Time, distance and size are other enemies of unity. Things are often not as they seem to be from our perspective on "our side of the river," as we look across time and distance at our brothers. When I first moved to Boston in 1987, many of the kingdom leaders either lived there or visited frequently. I could expect to see and talk to Kip McKean, Al Baird, Bob Gempel, Doug Arthur, Randy McKean and others on a fairly frequent basis. Things that bothered me would come up occasionally, and I could speak to any of these brothers to receive answers to my questions. I often found that what at first appearance bothered me would quickly be resolved. Now it can seem much harder to get answers and stay connected with brothers.

Time and distance can make our worlds seem separate and disunited. Reports from others about others often replace direct communication. I believe as never before that when things on the other side of the river concern us, it is even more crucial to make every effort to talk and to spend time together to resolve perceived differences. We must defeat the enemies of time, distance and size as they relate to unity. The larger we become as a kingdom, the more essential it will be to go to the other side of the river to maintain the unity God desires. One of the greatest strengths of our movement has been the commitment of our leaders to overcome these obstacles to preserve unity.

Fear

In my experience personally and in discipling others, one of the greatest enemies of unity is fear. In Joshua 22 the ten tribes feared that their brothers would get them in trouble, and the two and a half tribes feared that they would be forgotten by the larger group, the center of the "movement." They nearly destroyed each other because of fear.

Paul told Timothy, "God did not give us a spirit of timidity [or fear], but a spirit of power, of love and of self-discipline" (2 Timothy 1:7). As a young disciple and leader, I both loved and feared leaders in the kingdom. I wanted to serve and please them, but often felt afraid to say what I really felt, especially in the face of strong direction or challenge. This would lead to stuffing my thoughts or reactions, leaving leaders or disciplers unaware of how I felt. This also led to internal anxiety and stress in my thoughts and heart. Looking back, I think I confused fear with respect and loyalty.

Hard lessons followed when leaders I feared fell into sins and practices I had sensed and seen, but had been afraid to confront. I now realize that back then I approached older or more experienced leaders more as a child to a parent, rather than as a young adult to an older or more mature adult. I now believe my fear kept me from being used and taught by God in ways that could have spared myself and others much grief. I needed power, love and self-control to interact as an adult to an adult with those over, under and around me in the Lord. Fear keeps us from expressing gut reactions and feelings to those who can and must help us figure them out. Fear keeps us from learning to talk back respectfully but honestly. Fear also must be dealt with mutually by both sides of a relationship.

The ten tribes described in Joshua 22 did finally decide to go talk to the tribes on the other side of the river before going to war. Amazingly, they found out it all was a misunderstanding when they allowed their brothers to explain. How often have you made the same discovery once you decided to talk— and allowed others to as well? I believe this example of the stronger initiating with the weaker is a right and needed precedent in relational unity. The more mature should go first and take the greater responsibility when unity is threatened. John tells us:

> There is no fear in love. But perfect love drives out fear, because fear has to do with punishment. The one who fears is not made perfect in love. (1 John 4:18)

In this passage I have wondered who exactly *gives* the perfect love and then who exactly benefits from it. The word "perfect" means "mature." As I have matured, I have come to believe that mature leaders understand the extreme likelihood of fear in human relationships. They therefore seek to cast it out by being approachable, easy to talk to and understanding about people's feelings and fears, though they personally may not relate or may have long ago overcome what young Christians and young leaders are now experiencing.

With God, fear is the beginning of wisdom, but love is the stuff that maturity, confidence and longevity are built on. So it must be with people. When we are first building relationships with others, we are all intimidated and fearful of how they will treat us. This can even cause us to be on our "best behavior." But sooner or later, as with God, our unity with others must move to the honesty and openness of secure vulnerability based on the other's love and our self-control.

I have especially seen this proven true with my wife and kids. I grew up fearing my dad as much as I loved him. I saw my mom and siblings do the same. It was natural for me to assume that the same dynamic as a husband and father was normal in my family. However, my wife did not accept my anger and temper the way my mom had accepted my dad's. She reacted with honesty, hurt and openness about the fear I caused in her. She appealed for it not to be that way—and even had the nerve to share with others who discipled us about what I made her feel. I knew I did not want the greatest object of my heart's affection to fear me, but this alone did not cast it out.

Finally, a climactic breakthrough was achieved when one of my daughters caught me in the act of a rationalized temper tantrum with my wife. She simply stated, "Dad, when you get mad, you go to tone five, a mean face, and we are all scared to death." She went on to say, "It makes me not even want to live in the same house with you." My wife had shared similar things, but the combined message from her and the kids got to my heart. I went on a marriage getaway with my wife. With tears of conviction, I asked her to forgive me for my lack of love and maturity and for the damage my anger had produced through her fear. I promised to never justify my anger by pointing to her weaknesses (or even sins) again. I gave her permission to tell me whenever she felt any fear because of me. I promised that I would immediately stop talking and go pray for self-control and a loving spirit before continuing. My family will testify to the change in my character since that time.

Who do you fear, and who fears you? The answer to these questions is a beginning point for dramatic growth in godly unity, but recognition is only a beginning. You must go through the process of sharing your fear with those who can help cast it out. You must listen to the fear others have of you and get the conviction to cast it out of them by your repentance. I have reached a point in my own growth to generally not fear leaders, but to ask for mutual respect between us. God has taught me how to better control my own temptation to fear and to be able to look for it in others so that I can cast it out with my love. Mutual fear, rather than mutual love and respect, often lies at the heart of unity struggles in relationships. Overcoming fear with mature love defeats one of the greatest enemies of unity in all relationships.

Key Components for Unity

For some reason the words that come to mind when I think of key components of kingdom unity all begin with c.

Cause

I think first of our cause as a unifier among us. Followers of Jesus will only stay united with each other when Jesus' vision of knowing God, loving God, sharing our faith in God and glorifying God is the ultimate cause we are intellectually, emotionally, personally and mutually sold out to. The greatest commandment, the Great Commission, as well as Jesus' basic call to discipleship, all ask disciples to be champions of his cause. We are united in serving our Father and Brother and both lost and saved people, not just united in ideas and teaching. We seek to know Jesus and walk and talk like him. Our cause gives divine purpose and eternal definition to our unity and common sacrifice.

Convictions

Our convictions further define our unity. Paul spells out the foundational ones in Ephesians 4:1-6. We are united by the conviction that Jesus is our one Lord (meaning a relationship shared in common by all) and the conviction that there is one faith (a common set of teachings that can be understood and obeyed by all disciples). Paul goes on to speak of one baptism, the common baptism in water for forgiveness of sins that we each participated in to become Christians. He speaks of one Spirit, which we all received at baptism to empower our spiritual lives. Of course, there is one God and Father who is over all, through all and in all. Actually, first on his list is the one body, the body of Christ, which is his church. It is here that we are to "make every effort" to maintain "the unity of the Spirit through the bond of peace."

Unity is based on convictions, but maintained by "every" effort. In other words, believing the right things does not by itself keep us united. The enemies of unity will attack in spite of our convictions and be defeated only by an intensity of effort that includes phone calls, meetings, trips, money and agonizing effort to get to—and to understand—the other side of the river. I recall a meeting last year that required my wife and me to fly to Los Angeles on twenty-four hour's notice, along with other kingdom leaders, to sort through both theological and relational issues. We maintained unity and therefore all felt it was worth the effort.

Conscience

Conscience is yet another element crucial to unity. Baptism is cited as the pledge of a good conscience toward God in 1 Peter 3:21. Paul says a clear conscience is one of the fundamentals essential to the ultimate goal of the Christian faith (1 Timothy 1:5).

If I understand correctly, Romans 14 and 15 speak to the connection of conscience and unity in two ways. The first is that we all must stand before God individually, and our consciences and faith combine to allow or disallow us to feel right before God. The second is the recognition that one man's conscience and faith will be at a different place than another's. Herein lies the challenge and opportunity to forge unity: violation of our consciences constitutes sin on the individual's part, but causing another to violate his or her conscience by our conduct or attitude is not walking in love and is therefore sin against our brother or sister.

Conscience issues must be handled carefully. We must be slow to pull the conscience trigger against our brother's actions, for this restricts his freedom. On the other hand, we must respect the need of our brother's conscience and not run over him in the name of our freedom or of his needed education on a matter. Paul deals with food, days of worship and other things in Romans. For us, the issues have included wine, women's roles, music, and currently, raising and directing our kids, the movies we watch, materialistic standards, and using statistics and numbers in motivating leaders and ministry. Conscience considerations have been and will continue to be key components needed for unity and God's blessings. There must be room in our relationships for both sides of conscience issues as God moves us individually and collectively closer to his will.

Connections

Relational connection is also vital to unity. In Ephesians 4:11-16 Paul defines unity of the body of Christ as that which is held together by "every supporting ligament." From the context, these are leader and body relationships that support the unity of the whole from their individual roles and accompanying relationships. In traditional Churches of Christ, the term "autonomy" was used to cut off unwanted influence and input between congregations and their leaders and members. As in individual families, differences of leadership philosophy or implementation must be respected in our churches. However, in application, the Bible displays a very interactive and shared leadership connection. This is illustrated by the relationships between Peter, Paul, John and James in Galatians 2. The relationship between the Asian churches and Paul and his band of discipled evangelists, in which they came and went at Paul's direction or the church's request, also shows this connection. The early churches were connected by human personalities and their leadership roles.

Jesus is the only singular head of the church (Colossians 1:18). However apostles, evangelists, elders and teachers clearly formed a pool of collective leadership and unity that provided security, communication, conflict resolution and the ability to resolve internal issues before they destroyed unity. Paul's analogy of the fields on a farm and the servants who cultivate them (2 Corinthians 3:5-9) is my favorite description of the relational unity God's kingdom is to enjoy and exhibit. The servants are moved around to use their unique talents and strengths to supply portions of what God wants to provide a given church at a given time. It would appear that Peter, Apollos and Paul had each been used to work in the field in Corinth.

Acts 15 and the Jerusalem Council show how widespread struggles with unity were successfully handled among the churches because relational connection provided a collective wisdom and decision-making process that settled genuine questions and maintained unity. Acts 15:2 informs us that a "sharp dispute and debate" over circumcision occurred between disciples in Antioch. Unity, then or now, cannot be dictated. It must be forged. However, differences have to be resolved through a process that is understood and accepted. In this case, the negative aspect was not the dispute, but an unauthorized way of handling it (Acts 15:24). No one can argue that without the forged and connecting relationships of the apostles and elders, such issues would have divided the church. Perhaps we need an even better-developed process for conflict resolution among us today.

Our current roles, starting with world sector leaders and moving on through kingdom elders, teachers, geographic sector lead evangelists and more, provide healthy and needed connections to preserve and promote unity. I predict that we will need some "Jerusalem Councils" and contact (another c word!) in the years to come to maintain unity. As long as we value relational connections among us now, like they did in the first century, we will have what is needed to produce similar unifying results while facing potentially divisive issues. There have been and will be some bruised and strained ligaments that need to be healed and reunited among us. Our willingness and commitment to reconcile kingdom relationships may be one of the greatest tests of discipleship and of whether God is or is not with us. In John 17:20-21 Jesus prays for unity of disciples today when he says:

> "My prayer is not for them alone. I pray also for those who will believe in me through their message, that all of them may be one, Father just as you are in me and I am in you. May they also be in us so that the world may believe that you have sent me."

Companionship

Finally, companionship is a key to unity. Nothing inspired me more as a young Christian than the depth of love and friendship I saw Biblically in Jonathan and David, Paul and Timothy, or Jesus and John. I was also fired up by my personal companions who have truly become lifetime friends, transcending roles, ministry lines and responsibilities. Men like Sam Laing and Sam Powell, whose first name we chose for our first son, have long since gone from being disciplers or disciples to being lifetime best friends. Martin Bentley, Dan Allison,

Mitch Mitchell, Paul Ramsey, Bruce Williams, Doug Webber, Javier Amaya, Bud Chiles, Don Lee, Marty Wooten and many others, are men whom God brought me together with in the past. They have also become lifetime friends and eternal companions. They, and others like them, are no longer in my close circle of daily and functional roles, or friendships that sustain my spiritual and emotional needs. New best friends, like Gordon Ferguson, Dave Malutinok, Randy McKean, Dan Bathon, Jimmy Rogers, Bob Tranchell, Chip Mitchell and others in our world sector who are not on staff, have taken their places. But all these men are lifetime companions and friends in my journey toward heaven. I cherish their love, past or present connection, and friendship and would fight intensely to stay united in heart, spirit and fellowship with them. We have shared the battles of cause, conviction, conscience and connection and have become companions who look forward to spending an eternity of rest and joy together. There is a friend who sticks closer than a brother (Proverbs 18:24). I have many companions and friends whom I look forward to either welcoming or being welcomed as we all enter the company of Jesus in heaven.

Rewards of Unity

> How good and pleasant it is
>> when brothers live together in unity!
> It is like precious oil poured on the head,
>> running down on the beard,
> running down on Aaron's beard,
>> down upon the collar of his robes.
> It is as if the dew of Hermon
>> were falling on Mount Zion.
> For there the LORD bestows his blessing,
>> even life forevermore. (Psalm 133:1-3)

This passage in Psalms outlines reasons for valuing unity as disciples and as leaders. The emotional impact of unity on those who possess it is clearly stated here. God says that it is good and pleasant to live in unity. Many of us can vouch for how bad and depressing it is to live in strife, backbiting and conflict. Some of my darkest hours as a disciple have been while watching the pain and despair of conflict, bitterness and disunited relationships between disciples. Whether in marriages, families, discipling relationships or leadership circles, there is no worse experience than the aftermath of bitterness and unresolved conflict. Unity, on the other hand, brings life's most pleasant emotional experiences in relationships at all levels of life, as God intended. It must be valued in light of the positive and negative stakes involved for all, whether for our spouses, children, brothers, leaders or newest converts. God also says it is to unified believers that he gives his blessing. God will not bless any disunited group or situation. Unity and blessing go together like baptism and forgiveness of sin.

One of my favorite hymns has always been "When We All Get to Heaven." It depicts the exhilarating joy of the spiritual family reunion we will have with all those eternal best friends with whom we kept the unity of the Spirit and the bond of peace here on earth. Personally, I want both the emotional pleasantness and multiple blessings of Biblical unity!

12

Give Me the Bible!

F

Leadership and the Bible—now what would these have to do with each other? Of course I am being facetious; but we must ask ourselves how tightly connected these two are in our minds, our hearts and our practice. Truthfully, I went for a number of years in the movement not valuing deeper Bible study enough. I'm sure that this sounds strange coming from a person with reasonably in-depth formal Biblical training. In what we called a "preacher school," in a two-year, very intense setting, I took about forty courses in Bible and Biblical subjects. During that time, I memorized hundreds of verses, wrote dozens of research papers and took scores of exams. Later I attended graduate school and received a master of arts in New Testament studies. I also returned to teach in that preacher training school and taught something like twenty different courses, some of them again and again.

Why then would I have taken too lightly the need for more and better in-depth Biblical training for all leaders, as well as for young disciples? Basically because I came out of a legalistic religious group in which "knowledge puffs up" (1 Corinthians 8:1). I knew many leaders then who had a vast knowledge of the facts of the Bible, but whose character was malformed in spite of their learning. I also saw that their knowledge intellectually did not translate into practical applications that changed their lives, the lives of their families and the lives of the churches that they led. To be perfectly candid, I fell right into that same category—a knowledgeable person badly in need of discipling or training. Therefore, once I became a part of those seriously committed to discipleship and evangelism, I just wanted to learn the practicals I had missed, almost to the exclusion of trying to increase my own Biblical knowledge.

The Need for More

With the passing of only a few years, my concerns began to grow about where we were generally as a movement in our Biblical knowledge. Unless we are excited about learning the deeper truths of the Bible on a continual basis, we lose an alarming amount of spiritual motivation—and substitute worldly motivation in its place. Many of our more mature leaders obtained systematic Biblical training of one type or another, and while they appreciate the training, I am not sure that they understand what those without it are really missing. Without good Bible training, a spiritual crisis will develop. Your church may be in that crisis mode right now. If the average disciple does not deepen his or her Biblical root system, each is going to have a difficult time hanging on to God when the storms of life are raging. My son once told me that during his times of struggle as a young single man, he knew too much Bible from his youth to seriously contemplate leaving God. Evidently, many other Christians do not have that same grounding.

Leaders, especially those on the ministry staff, are not going to be able to take their ministries higher without taking them deeper at the same time. Yet, in our shortsightedness, some manifest the attitude: "Don't worry about it, just baptize some people." Even while on death row, Paul told Timothy to "bring...my scrolls, especially the parchments" (2 Timothy 4:13). Is this the kind of thirst for knowledge that you have? Some leaders are shallow Biblically. This may be why the more mature in our audiences are not enthralled with their preaching. Thankfully, most of us seem to want to drink more deeply, but when I encounter a prominent but lazy-minded leader, I find that he can negatively influence other staff members with the same plague. Let's just repent and imitate Paul by digging deeper and infusing all of those in our charge to likewise be excited about learning.

Let me describe a scenario that is all too common among us. Sunday morning sermons are often primarily dedicated to reaching the non-Christian. Midweek services typically consist of three basic components: contribution, announcements and a brief lesson that is designed to promote evangelism (i.e. we need more visitors for Sunday). Where are our people going to get the Biblical diet that they so desperately need? Even if we determine to use Sundays as our primary visitor outreach, which may or may not be wise in a given cultural setting, at least half of the sermon should be aimed at disciples. For that part, more depth and more variety is needed. Some of us are so predictable that the veterans in the audience could finish our illustrations for us and predict fairly accurately which Scriptures we are going to use. There is a word for that: *Boring!* Midweek services should have as a major component Biblical teaching that is carefully planned out for distinct purposes and then carefully prepared for by our own study. How much time do you spend working on your Sunday sermon? How much time do you spend working on your midweek lesson? I spend more time on the latter than the former, primarily because of the necessary depth of a lesson designed solely for disciples' growth.

Other means of teaching the Bible must be utilized besides these regular lesson times. Special teaching days with guest teachers are highly effective. A series on Saturday mornings is another possibility—a revival of the old STP (Spiritual Training Program) approach. Sunday school classes for adults before worship services are a good means for teaching more Bible. Of course, the common concern voiced about this possibility is that it makes getting visitors to services more unwieldy. This is true, but the difficulty does not automatically dismiss the possibility.[1] Guided studies using cassette tape series taught by

---

[1] It does, however, provide some additional impetus for reconsidering whether Sundays should be our main evangelistic push for the week.

kingdom teachers and others (available through DPI) give us other possible ways to get our people into the Scriptures.

More and more computer-related training is becoming available, with the Biblical Resource Center (BRC) leading the way. This approach was developed under the direction of Marty Wooten and Steve Staten and utilizes a CD-ROM presentation of teachers in the kingdom lecturing on key subjects. As you watch the teacher delivering his lessons, you also see the exact text of his speech just under him, with an extended outline out to the side. The technology is impressive, and as more courses become available, they deserve to be widely used by all disciples, especially leaders. (I am scheduled to do at least one course in the coming months, as are other kingdom teachers.)

This is not intended to be an exhaustive list, but only a quick mention of a few possibilities that hopefully will stimulate your thinking and help you figure out additional means of promoting deeper Bible study among your group. Given the patterns we have had for a number of years, leaders will not find it easy to put these things into practice. But we need the conviction that this is something that must be done.

What Must We Preach?

A well-rounded diet is a must. In chapter 8 I discuss striking a balance in several key areas of our teaching program. Recently, Randy McKean taught a lesson at a leadership retreat that was both challenging and thrilling. One key premise was that we preach so much on evangelism that we end up with an emphasis not to be found in the Bible. Other things are emphasized that result in evangelism. Sometimes certain results are best arrived at as a by-product of our emphases. For example, if we go out in search of happiness, we are not likely to find it. On the other hand, if we go out seeking to please God, we find happiness every time.

Randy shared many verses that point out the need to emphasize these key subjects (note the order):

God
Jesus
love
heaven
mission

If we love God and his Son with all our hearts, the church as ourselves, and have our eyes set on the unseen (2 Corinthians 4:17-18), evangelism will follow. Or will it? Are we simply dreaming at this point and heading down an unproven path?

Doug Arthur recently delivered a lesson at a leadership conference that made much the same point as Randy's lesson. Doug used Acts 2:42-47 to make his case. It is a familiar passage, to be sure, but look carefully at it once more.

> They devoted themselves to the apostles' teaching and to the fellowship, to the breaking of bread and to prayer. Everyone was filled with awe, and many wonders and miraculous signs were done by the apostles. All the believers were together and had everything in common. Selling their possessions and goods, they gave to anyone as he had need. Every day they continued to meet together in the temple courts. They broke bread in their homes and ate together with glad and sincere hearts, praising God and enjoying the favor of all the people. And the Lord added to their number daily those who were being saved.

Notice the sequence of what happened. After the three thousand were baptized (v41), they were devoted to four things: the apostles' teaching, fellowship, communion and prayer. The result of this devotion was that everyone loved being together, even daily; they were willing to sell their possessions and share them with one another; they continually praised God; and people were being saved daily. The text does not say that they were devoted to the Great Commission or to evangelism. They were devoted to body life, and by their deep love for one another and unity with each other as family, Jesus' words in John 13:34-35 and John 17:20-23 were fulfilled. In addition, listen to the words of the prophet Isaiah:

> You who bring good tidings to Zion,
>   go up on a high mountain.
> You who bring good tidings to Jerusalem,
>   lift up your voice with a shout,
> lift it up, do not be afraid;
>   say to the towns of Judah,
>   "Here is your God!" (Isaiah 40:9)

The chapter goes on to describe God in heart-thrilling ways. We need to see God. If we focus on man and his problems, we will lose faith; if we focus on God and his power, we will gain faith. Shouting loudly that we need more faith does absolutely nothing to build it. Showing God to people is the means to that essential end—but we cannot keep using the same twenty passages. Dig into the Bible—all of it—and come up with golden nuggets that people may have missed. Lift up God, lift up Jesus, paint a picture of heaven, and then tell people how to respond appropriately to that vision.

The day I wrote this chapter, I preached a lesson about building family by seeing God as Father. Many people, including the leader's wife, told me that they were starving for such a lesson, such a picture of God. People all through the audience were brushing back tears—not because of my oratorical skills, but because they were seeing God. All I did was determine that I would pour out all of my energies and heart to try as best I could to point them to the love of a Father who deeply wants a relationship with them. When was the last time in your audience you saw tears that were produced by helping people to see God? Making people cry with stories of a baby starving or dying is one thing, but making people cry over seeing God is yet another. Human-interest stories have their place, but too many of us do not know how to use Scripture to move the hearts of God's people.

Do you need to break out of your mold, to break away from the same old approach to preaching? It is never too late to dig deep and learn how to help others dig deeper. Whatever fills your heart will fill the hearts of others. For example, I heard Douglas Jacoby talk about a survey of his home ministry, in which he asked how many books people had read in the past year. He commented that only a few people in his group, not just staff, had read one hundred books or more. Good grief, Charlie Brown! How in the world do you motivate *anyone* to read one hundred books in a year? Only by doing it. Douglas does it about every year, and those who are around him read far, far more than the average person among us. What is the point? If you are going to get others to excitedly dig into the Bible, you need to model it. Preaching about what you are not doing will fall flat in its effect. The Holy Spirit cannot bless hypocrisy. If you are not doing it, do not preach it. Of course, you can repent and preach it, but some of us keep "repenting" of the same things without changing. Those listening to this broken record are no longer moved by it. This cycle robs those under our leadership of their faith.

Don't Get Too Fancy

Years ago, I visited the most fruitful campus ministry group in the "old" campus ministry movement. I expected the preacher to be a very charismatic speaker on whom our eyes would be riveted as he mesmerized us with his wit and oratory genius. I could not have been more surprised. He simply opened the Bible and went verse by verse through most of a chapter, making very pointed applications of the principles, with very little hoopla otherwise. He was light on drama, light on humor, light on illustrations, but heavy on Bible. He was so serious about the Bible that most everyone else was also. What he had done in that traditional setting was amazing, and the reverence he and his audience had for the word of God is not often equaled. Yes, there were some sins in that situation which led to the demise of that very ministry, but for many years prior, the results almost defied description for that era. The Bible was taught in many settings throughout the average week, and some of our top leaders today are products of that phenomenon.

We are sometimes afraid to just teach the Bible. We think that we have to perform or entertain. We need a mind change on this one. We need to trust the power of the Word. Isaiah 55:8-11 assures us that God's word will accomplish what he sends it out to accomplish. We could fill this book with quotations about the power of the Word, but do we really believe it?

Read Nehemiah 8 for a real shocker about devotion to the Word. The people stood up while Ezra the scribe read the Bible from daybreak until noon, and it says (v3) that all the people listened attentively as he read. Amazing! "Well, our people have short attention spans and could never do anything like that." Do you really think that these people naturally had an attention span that made this accomplishment easy? What I think is that their leaders, Ezra and Nehemiah, had a view of God and Scripture themselves that inspired the people to go far beyond their normal capacity to reverence the Word. Hearts transfer. Many positive spiritual attributes that our people have in them came from us as leaders. Conversely, many of the negative attributes remain in them because of a lack of leadership example, inspiration and training from us. We must own this one and repent ourselves of not hungering for a deeper knowledge of the Bible before we will be able to effectively call them higher. Are you ready to do this? I am. I believe what I am saying, but I am guilty along with you. We simply must change. Let's do it, and let's do it now. And may God truly be lifted up as a result!

13

Handling Life's Transitions with Grace

S

Nowhere is the application of the Golden Rule more needed than when we or our fellow disciples are going through major life transitions. I am referring here to such events as moving, changing roles, sickness, the empty nest, a friend falling away, the aging of our parents, a family member leaving the Lord, and the like. It has long been observed that disciples are much more likely to fall away or to do poorly spiritually when such things are happening. "Do to others as you would have them do to you" takes on critical emotional implications in such situations.

Transitions almost always involve more than one disciple effecting the transition or being affected by it. In a transition each person affected needs to be identified, understood and then responded to in Christlike or Golden Rule fashion. At the very least there is the one in transition *and* the significant person or people who are responsible for both how they feel and are treated during and after. For instance, when someone comes out of the ministry, there is the primary leader who made the hard decision *and* the one coming out. Often, transitions involve multiple parties who are affected. Again, using the ministry staff transition as an illustration, there is the family who is coming off staff, the ministry they are no longer leading, the peers they have been leading with and even non-Christians who want to know what happened. *How people are treated at such critical times are tests of our love, maturity and understanding of God and Jesus.* Whether or not people feel the Golden Rule being applied at such times will either be a major stumbling block or a tremendous boost to their confidence in our fellowship.

Apply the Rule

I want first to break down what the Golden Rule involves so we can know how to practice it, and then to show how to apply it in some of the above situations. "Do to others" implies that we are going to deliberately act on someone else's behalf. It begins with denial of our own needs and feelings, then taking time, energy and effort to invest in others. "As you would have them do to you" means we must first put ourselves in the other person's place. This is harder than we often admit, primarily because all of us are more self-centered than we think. It means that our busy-ness has to be focused on someone else's business.

I must carefully consider how something that has happened to another person would affect me, how it would make me feel and what it would leave me to deal with in its wake if it had happened to me. This process leads to empathy, sympathy and a better understanding of what a person needs in such circumstances. To think this way is to be like Jesus—which he wants us to be, far more often than we are.

Having put ourselves in the other person's place, we can much more easily think of a course of action or something to say, as well as some things we would *not* want said or done. Sometimes we miss the Golden Rule by doing or saying nothing. More often, we probably miss the mark by doing or saying something without thinking about how it will sound or feel to the other person. For example, my dad and mom are going through a tough time right now as they deal with issues related to growing old. I find myself needing to really consider what is best to say and do, and I can only do this by thinking about what I will want when I am at their point in life. To live out the Golden Rule, we all have to take time to go to the other side and walk in others' shoes. Now let's make some applications to specific situations.

Role Changes

Jesus said "a man's life does not consist in the abundance of his possessions" (Luke 12:15). He no doubt said this after observing the importance that people attach to things. It is equally apparent how much importance we attach to roles that often define who we are and determine our self-esteem. I have personally felt self-doubt that grows out of concern for my image and what others think about my worth as they view what I do. We have all wrestled with how what we do reflects on who we are. Therefore, we should realize that role changes often create a need for Golden Rule treatment of others.

Changes caused by perceived or real failures of some kind or negative assessments of capability are the hardest to take. These can occur in school, dating, marriage, family, career or other arenas such as sports or the arts. We must initially respond to friends or disciples in such circumstances by both thinking about and asking how it makes them feel. Put yourself in their place and go through what you would feel if the tables were turned. *This takes deliberate effort, especially when our current roles are secure and comfortable.*

I suggest three ways that you can help. First, acknowledging pain is usually a good place to start when people are hurting. This at least shows you are trying to relate to them. We all appreciate empathy and sympathy.

Second, helping people to get perspective is encouraging when they are going through painful changes. Jesus was actually giving perspective in the above scripture to someone who was worried about loss of possessions. Loss of role also has to be seen for what it is and isn't. A role is not one's life or what makes life worth living. Roles are replaceable. God can provide ways to fulfill us other than the way we have been working, relating or participating. Often when people come out of the ministry, they have been assuming that this role was the most important they could ever have. God does not think this way, but rather, insists that all roles in the body of Christ are equally important (Romans 12; 1 Corinthians 12; Ephesians 4). He can provide other means of income and of impact.

Many changes that we go through are some form of God's discipline, according to Hebrews 12:10-11, but they are never meant to harm us; rather, they are intended to make us better—more holy, righteous and mature. The more attached we are to people or positions, the more painful our changes of role are. Often God is teaching us to rely more on him than on "them," and the *short-term* pain is a means to *long-term* gain. As I look back on my life, I have changed roles in terms of position, title, location and people I was close to many times. I can now see that God was training me to become more of who I am today as an elder, evangelist, geographic HOPE leader, husband and father. My perspective is that the pain was always worth the gain when I surrendered to God's purpose and process. It helps people to know that we relate to their pain, but that we remember the gains and realize the progress that God intended long after the pain is gone.

Finally, people need to feel that our *agape* for them is not limited to our role or theirs, but is unconditional and lasting. This is sometimes the most difficult step in treating others as we would want to be treated. Certainly roles do affect frequency of contact and interaction. If you stop dating someone steadily, contact will be affected; but I believe in this tough transition, Christians can still be committed to what is best for each other and to love unconditionally, though not romantically.

The greatest fear most people have with regard to role changes is about what the future will hold. We must assure them that there are no unreconciled relationship issues. Acceptance and appreciation for the person and his or her past and future value to us needs to be expressed. Ongoing communication and support needs to put action behind these words of promised loyalty and love. For ministry leaders this should affect how we treat people who come out of ministry roles by maintaining friendship and contact after the role changes. The change is a test not only for the one going off staff but also for those who continue on after they depart. The temptation is to allow weirdness about the change to prevent a natural friendship from transcending the roles. It can feel awkward to be around each other under the new dynamics. New topics of conversation are in order, which take thoughtfulness and consideration—more so than the ones that flowed out of our shared work dynamic. We must push through the awkwardness and focus on the many convictions and similar circumstances and dynamics of life and discipleship that are still shared. We all still eat and enjoy meals, fellowship, fun activities and hobbies, sports events or recreation. The key is demonstrating the effort and forethought to set up opportunities that used to occur because of working together and now have to be more deliberately arranged.

I have close friends who once shared a staff ministry role with me that I now share Bible studies, a date, a meal or a fishing trip with. In some of these cases, I had to repent because at first I let the weirdness win rather than the Golden Rule and true friendship. Let's make sure our relationships in Jesus transcend any roles and that our love is really deep and from the heart—not shallow and based on schedules and jobs that brought us together.

Gordon recently returned from Triangle, North Carolina, where he spoke on the book of Romans for the church there. When he returned to Boston, he brought with him a large carton of my favorite barbecue sent by John and Michaela Iiames. The Iiameses once served with Jeanie and me in the ministry here in Boston. John now has a great job with the federal EPA, and Michaela teaches school. We are very excited that they will be returning to Boston next summer for John to get his doctorate in forestry at the University of New Hampshire. Our friendship has only grown over the years since their transition. That barbecue tasted great, not just because it was from North Carolina but because it represented a gift from a friendship that transcends our roles.

Al and Gloria Baird have always been role models for me in how to treat people after transitions. They still call Jeanie and me on our birthdays and our anniversary long after the roles that kept us in close contact have changed. Spiritual friends can truly be friends forever, regardless of roles.

When People Leave God

We have recently introduced an entire ministry focused on the recovery of weak Christians, seeking to prevent them from leaving the Lord. But when a person does turn away, it presents all of us with emotional, relational and philosophical dilemmas. The Bible is always the best place to turn when we need clarity and direction. In Luke 15, several parables are taught by Jesus that reveal God's heart for people who were found but have again become lost. In each, the first message is that they are to receive a high priority, above that shown to those who are still found. Disciples should always assume that the fallen brother or sister needs to be found. This does not mean that all who leave will greet our efforts with joy or gratitude. But you can be sure that if we fail to pursue them, they will read this as a lack of love and caring—which it is. At times of spiritual weakness, people can confuse us with their verbal or nonverbal messages. Like us, they may not be rational or appreciative at these times, just as a sick person often lacks these qualities when needing medical attention. Doctors are not trained to give their best effort only to rational or appreciative patients, but to *sick* patients, whatever their demeanor might be.

Another lesson seen in these parables is acceptance. The father accepted the fact that his younger son could leave and did not try to force him to stay. This does not mean he did not care for him or appeal for him not to leave, but that he respected his right to choose. This actually allows the son to see how he must dwell in the father's house of his own volition. It also leads him to take more personal responsibility when his life caves in and to realize how good he had it at home. Christians who have left God need to undergo this same process. There should be pursuit but not pressure, as with the father in the parable.

The return of his son seems to be something the father anticipated and planned for. I am sure that, in his mind, he had thrown that most joyful of parties many times. The ring, robe and cow had been given in his heart many times over as he prayed for and awaited his son's return. We too must have hope and also give hope for the return of prodigals among us. They are not to be strangers we have forgotten about or objects of resentment for the pain they caused in leaving. The parable shows how to practice the Golden Rule of treating those who have left as we would want to be treated if we ourselves had left. Their return should be the focus of our hearts and prayers, and the party should already be planned in our minds. Recently, the daughters of two close friends of mine each returned to God. I had the privilege of sharing in the restoration process. Their restorations were as sweet—if not sweeter—than their baptisms. On another occasion, I had to help a family remember this parable, as they were consumed with how to prevent their prodigal daughter from leaving again rather than rejoicing at her return. We cannot control when or whether people leave, but we can determine how much they feel welcomed and accepted when they return. Let's practice the Golden Rule on this one.

I believe it is equally important to practice the Golden Rule when close brothers or sisters have a family member or close friend who falls away. Nothing hurts more than to feel the loss of someone close to home. Again, we need to share their pain, but most of all, focus on the above principles from the parable. Disciples will either draw comfort and faith or despair and faithlessness from the way their brothers and sisters respond at such crucial times. We need to point them to the parables of Luke 15 and the principles of how to respond with faith, hope and love. We need to join with them in prayer and anticipation of the return, rather than focusing on the leaving. These parables teach us that people will leave the kingdom—and also come back. Let's apply the Golden Rule both to those who leave and to the brothers and sisters who are close to them.

Aging Parents

"Honor your father and mother" is one of the ten commandments, and it is reinforced by Paul in 1 Timothy 5:5-16, where he teaches that anyone who does not take care of his own family is worse than an unbeliever. Many of us in the kingdom are reaching the stage in life when our parents are aging and are approaching death. None of us will fully understand what it is like to grow old until we experience the process itself. However, all of us can practice the Golden Rule by anticipating the process and seeking to give grace and love to our parents as God would have it. The aging of our parents will present both opportunities and challenges in our relationships with them and with our siblings (for those who have them).

Our parents actually become more dependent on us—as we once were on them. Siblings will wrestle with everything from unresolved feelings of the past to the sharing of financial, emotional and physical loads of caretaking. Difficult choices related to health care, assisted versus unassisted living, timing of the sale of homes, when to stop driving, funeral arrangements and financial choices, will have to be negotiated with wisdom, love and patience by all. I have gone through this process with close friends like Gordon, and Bob and Pat Gempel and their parents, and now I am in the middle of it personally, as my own parents are more than eighty years old and in declining health.

The anticipation of losing them is real and emotional at unexpected times. My dad recently gave me his shotgun. I put it away in my gun cabinet here in Massachusetts and tears welled up as I remembered all the special moments in the woods that he and I had shared that will never be repeated. I am feeling those emotions even as I write, because no one else has his place in my heart or history. It has been good to share these feelings with Jeanie and other close friends like Gordon who can relate and give me perspective. Gordon lost his dad with whom he shared many of the same type of memories and moments growing up. I shared these feelings with my dad and let him know how special such times with him had been and how they will be remembered. We all need to let such feelings out (whether happy or sad) and figure out which are appropriate to share with our parents, siblings or close spiritual friends. We don't have to go through the process personally to begin anticipating it and being sensitized to how we can treat our friends or brothers and sisters when they go through it.

The Bible is once again our best source of wisdom and insight, teaching us to accept aging as a normal, necessary reality (Ecclesiastes, Proverbs). We are commanded to treat our parents with honor, regardless of how they treated us. The emotions of grief, loss and acceptance will need to be experienced, empathized with and understood by us and for others. The Golden Rule will be very much needed and appreciated in these challenging times.

Dating Relationships

One of the most challenging transitions to handle with grace (and to help others with) is the breakup of a dating relationship. Phil Arsenault has a challenge for any teen who considers the possibility of steady dating. He simply asks if the teen can handle "the breakup test." Simply put, he is asking them to consider the emotional risk of getting hurt before they invest in the relationship at that level of commitment. The saying, "No pain, no gain," is often never truer than in dating relationships, even in the kingdom. Baptism does not make us immune to hurting or being hurt in male-female relationships. However, the value of dating other disciples can be seen in many short-term and long-term results when it is done with advice, counsel, honesty and humility.

In the Old Testament the phrase "in the course of time" is often used to describe how time brings with it many transitions—some of which we control, but some of which we just have to deal with. We all experience "the course of time" and the many transitions it brings into our own lives and the lives of those around us. Jesus taught that the Golden Rule is a safety net of emotional support that all of us provide and all of us rely upon in the course of time. Let us appreciate both the need and opportunity we will have to practice this tool of God's grace and have others practice it for our benefit. Many other transitions could be discussed but hopefully this chapter will help us find God's plan for graceful transitions in our own lives and to make it available to many others.

14

Remember the Poor
A Charge to Leaders

S

Chip Mitchell, our campus evangelist, recently made an excellent point during a sermon from John 13:29, "Since Judas had charge of the money, some thought Jesus was telling him to buy what was needed for the feast, or to give something to the poor." Chip observed that the first assumption people had about Jesus spending money was that he was either (1) taking care of the disciples or (2) serving the poor. These acts of kindness were his reputation, his pattern.

Having learned from the Master, Peter, James, John, Paul and Barnabas were eager to carry out the same kindness to the poor:

> James, Peter and John, those reputed to be pillars, gave me and Barnabas the right hand of fellowship when they recognized the grace given to me. They agreed that we should go to the Gentiles, and they to the Jews. All they asked was that we should continue to remember the poor, the very thing I was eager to do. (Galatians 2:9-10)

Significantly, remembering the poor was the final subject of conversation as they discussed dividing up world evangelism among one another. All four of these early church leaders were "eager" to "continue to remember the poor" (Galatians 2:10), implying that they each were already doing this as individual disciples of Jesus.

In the New Millennium

As I write this, I am on the second leg of a return flight from Delhi, India. The meeting of the vice presidents for HOPE *worldwide* was held there, during which we visited a leprosy village, a computer school and an orphanage—each built and run for the poor by disciples. At the Village of HOPE more than 4,000 leprosy patients and their families live in houses built by disciples who freely gave their money and continue to give their service of love, in terms of medical attention, education and friendship. This week, it was incredibly moving to walk among the leprosy patients there, especially as I remembered financially giving to this cause years ago at a worship service held in the old Boston Garden. Seeing the wounds of the leprosy patients washed by disciples, I recalled Jesus' words in Matthew 10:7-8:

> "As you go, preach this message: 'The kingdom of heaven is near.' Heal the sick, raise the dead, cleanse those who have leprosy, drive out demons. Freely you have received, freely give."

Freely the Indian disciples have received and freely they have given back to the poor as they go about imitating Jesus and the apostles.

Hand in Hand

While at the Village of HOPE, I visited the house of the parents of one of our brothers, a man who became a disciple himself because he saw the compassion of Jesus through the disciples. He now serves on the HOPE staff at the village, remembering the poor as he spreads the good news of Jesus.

Remembering the poor and preaching the gospel go together because this was the ministry of Jesus and the apostles—and must be the lifestyle of disciples of Jesus today:

> Jesus went through all the towns and villages, teaching in their synagogues, preaching the good news of the kingdom and healing every disease and sickness. When he saw the crowds, he had compassion on them, because they were harassed and helpless, like sheep without a shepherd. (Matthew 9:35-36)

Around the globe, the volunteer work of disciples is opening doors for the gospel, as our unconditional love shows others how much we care, which leads the way to sharing what we know about the truth of the gospel.

For example, there are now more than 5,000 members of the International Churches of Christ in India. The vast majority have been converted since Douglas Arthur preached a powerfully convicting message about serving the poor at a world missions conference back in 1987. The mission work in India had gone slowly until Mark Templer and other Indian church leaders put this heart-changing message into practice, and God began to increase disciples in a much more dramatic fashion.

Seeing the church work and HOPE work in India so intricately intertwined gave me fresh conviction about remembering the poor. As a church leader myself, I am more committed to do so, and I call all disciples around the world to continue to remember the poor more and more.

The Heart of the Matter

Despite my desire to be like Jesus, when I was first asked to lead the HOPE Worldwide work in our world sector, I was not thrilled with the idea. It challenged my heart to consider myself in a primary role of serving the poor. Perhaps because we men tend to draw much self-esteem from what we do and how our job reflects on our identity, I would even get defensive when asked by an old friend in the ministry how I was handling my transition to HOPE. I could tell from their questions that they too would have struggled if asked to do the same.

I knew that I had to go to God's word to change my heart. As I studied my Bible, I was amazed at the volume of Scripture that is devoted to our attitude and efforts toward the poor. I soon realized that God was not just testing *my* heart with devotion to the poor, but he tests every disciple's heart. I'm sure that others would struggle with a role change—like I did—because we all carry more prejudice than we realize toward our fellow human beings. The term "Ugly American" has been given to our nation's citizenry abroad in part because, as the most blessed nation, we do not have the matching reputation of being the most humble nation. With our privilege has not come gratitude toward God for his blessings. How we think and act toward the poor are great litmus tests of our own humility.

I realized that my main reaction toward spearheading the HOPE work for our world sector was personal pride and prejudice toward being associated with less "successful" types of people. James addresses this favoritism bias very directly in a book that, perhaps better than any other, defines practical spirituality:

> My brothers, as believers in our glorious Lord Jesus Christ, don't show favoritism. Suppose a man comes into your meeting wearing a gold ring and fine clothes, and a poor man in shabby clothes also comes in. If you show special attention to the man wearing fine clothes and say, "Here's a good seat for you," but say to the poor man, "You stand there" or "Sit on the floor by my feet," have you not discriminated among yourselves and become judges with evil thoughts?
>
> Listen, my dear brothers: Has not God chosen those who are poor in the eyes of the world to be rich in faith and to inherit the kingdom he promised those who love him? But you have insulted the poor. Is it not the rich who are exploiting you? Are they not the ones who are dragging you into court? Are they not the ones who are slandering the noble name of him to whom you belong? (James 2:1-7)

In the first century, as in the twenty-first, disciples were tempted with valuing a rich man over a poor one. Favoritism was found in their fellowship in very discernable ways, as they treated the well-off better than the needy—even among their own brothers. Today it may not be favoritism in our seating arrangements, but perhaps in who we ask to speak in front of the church or who we are quicker to fellowship with. In greeting visitors, are we quicker to notice those dressed nicely or the ones more poorly dressed? It is convicting to know that God visited the planet as a carpenter and many had a hard time accepting him because of what he did, where he came from and even what he looked like (Isaiah 53:2).

Since accepting my role as a geographic HOPE leader, I have grown in not shrinking back from the stench and filth of slums, from dirty faces, hands or hugs of orphans, from sick, dying people and frail seniors. While on earth, Jesus championed the cause of the needy, not just the spiritually needy but the physically, emotionally and educationally needy. Who are we more comfortable with, the wealthy or the needy, the pretty or the undesirable? Are we willing to reach out and touch the leper's sores, the orphan's runny nose, the senior's dirty bib or diaper (yes, diaper)? Are we willing to let an orphan mess up our house, our schedule and even our free time—or the early arrival of our empty nest? Some dread the empty nest, but others relish it too highly.

I am not trying to decide what you need to change, but I am boldly stating that many among us need to be confronted with our attitudes and prejudices toward the needy. We in the kingdom, like most Americans, can be tempted to highly value beauty, education, athletic ability and wealth. This can lead us to favor those who possess such things and push our children toward exalting and striving for such things. While doing our best in every area for the glory of God is right, it is in serving the poor and needy that we often are tested as to whether we value the things of man more than the things of God (Luke 16:14-15).

Some Practicals

As I study the abundance of Scripture on the subject, I see an emphasis on several aspects of serving the poor which I believe should guide our efforts personally and collectively. God knows who and where the poor are and what each one needs, and he wants to use each one of us to meet these needs—from leaders to the newest disciples. Nothing softens our hearts like helping those in need. As leaders, we need to be personally involved and not just delegate our responsibility to others.

As We Go

Simply helping those in need as we come upon them, wherever we go, is the first practical way of serving. In Luke 10, just after sending out the Twelve (as seen in Matthew 10 above), Jesus told the Parable of the Good Samaritan, which fits in with what disciples should be doing as we go about preaching the good news. In this parable Jesus was also answering the question, "What must I do to inherit eternal life?" (Luke 10:25), which shows that serving our needy neighbors is fundamental to our salvation. The crux of the parable is that our neighbor is anyone in need whom we pass along the daily road of life.

In India I was nearly overwhelmed by the poverty I saw around me everywhere I went. It was easy to put this parable into practice by pulling out money or food at nearly any street corner to feed the hungry children or crippled beggars. It was also easy to observe how many other people passed them by without a word, except maybe "Be gone!" or "Get away from my car." Jesus would surely preach this parable on the streets of Delhi again and again. But what about in the suburbs of America or Great Britain or on the impressive streets of Paris or Buenos Aries: Do we practice this parable there?

I was convicted recently when my neighbor came over and used his snowblower on my driveway before I had ever done any act of kindness for him. Who is your neighbor? Do you stop to meet his or her need, or do you pass by on the other side of your busy street of daily life? The brothers and sisters in India have come to the conviction that serving the poor and needy should be a part of counting the cost with those who are becoming disciples. If those in such an obviously needy nation are being called to this conviction, how much more should those of us in more comfortable situations be called to the same?

Orphans, Widows and Aliens

Another specific focus of God's love is found in Deuteronomy 10:18-19:

> He defends the cause of the fatherless and the widow, and loves the alien, giving him food and clothing. And you are to love those who are aliens, for you yourselves were aliens in Egypt.

The cause of the fatherless, widow and alien is championed by God and mandated for us, his people. There are an estimated twenty million orphans in the world, and the number of widows and elderly unable to fend for themselves is even greater.

Orphans need families, love and a future. I believe many disciple families should be planned with adoption or foster care as a goal. It is not for everyone, but everyone is to have God's heart toward helping these needy children, ensuring that they feel God's love from each of us. What are you personally doing to help orphans?

Widows and seniors need quality time, respect, dignity and acts of service. If God allows it, we will each age and go through the difficult effects of it one day. Americans are youth worshipers, but Hollywood and cosmetics cannot stop the hand of physical degeneration. Those who do unto others who are old when we are young are more likely to find mercy and grace when we need it. Do we even know who the widows are in our neighborhood and stop to ask if we could shop or shovel snow for them? And how do we treat seniors among us? Do we show them love, respect and attention, as we will want when our turn comes?

Aliens or immigrants (as we may better know them as) are often mistreated, mistrusted and undesired in their new culture. Disciples are to live as foreigners and aliens to the world (1 Peter 2:11) and can therefore relate and show compassion to those feeling the same things physically which we feel spiritually. They need Christlike care, provision and friendship. They need our money, technology, mentoring and involvement in their lives.

Americans and those in other first world countries are the wealthiest people in the world in terms of how many have more than most elsewhere. We are those to whom much has been given and from whom much will be required, especially in giving to others as God has given to us (see Luke 12:48). We must ask ourselves that if we were the have-nots of the world, where would we look for help? We must do unto others as we would have them do unto us if roles were reversed. The inner cities of many first world countries are often populated with higher proportions of orphans, widows, seniors and aliens who are all special to God. We need more programs of volunteer involvement with these groups. The needy will always be with us in this world—at home and abroad (Mark 14:7). The question is whether we will do unto them as we would have them do unto us if the roles were reversed. How can we lead like Jesus if we don't champion the cause of the poor and the needy?

Disciples around the world have responded eagerly to serving the poor through special events, fund raising and in some cases, giving up their first world comforts to serve the poor in the third world. I am proud of the responsiveness and example we are beginning to set in serving the poor as a brotherhood and as individuals. Let us lead our people in this area so that every disciple has the heart of serving the poor and needy on a day-to-day basis.

15

How Shall We Lead?

S

This book has been an effort to share our understanding, experience, observations and time-seasoned convictions about leadership in God's kingdom. It certainly is not exhaustive and should not be read as the final word on the subject. It is simply our current outlook on what is Biblical and what is not, what works long-term with people and what does not. It contains what we believe are the most crucial elements of successfully leading people for Jesus in our day.

God continues to move among his people by exposing, enlightening and guiding us to a better understanding of his revealed truths. High turnover rates among our leadership would seem to indicate that some of our past ways of motivating and building ministries are showing unhealthy side effects. We have been part of both the good and the bad of our past practices and are not pointing fingers of criticism; but hopefully the insights we are sharing will be beneficial to us all. This book summarizes some of our most significant conclusions in hope that these will stimulate wholesome thinking, evaluation and changes as needed. To me, the following elements are the most crucial for becoming Golden Rule leaders and producing disciples who joyfully follow as we lead them to faithful, fruitful, enduring and happy lives.

Principle and Integrity

> They came to him and said, "Teacher, we know you are a man of integrity. You aren't swayed by men, because you pay no attention to who they are; but you teach the way of God in accordance with the truth. Is it right to pay taxes to Caesar or not?" (Mark 12:14)

Jesus is the ultimate example of leadership, and his reputation, even among critics, provides insight as to what he valued and exemplified as a leader. He was known as a man of integrity first and foremost. Integrity is a conscientious and firm adherence to a code or standard of values. It has to do with putting principle ahead of personality or position (whether others' or our own). Jesus was not swayed by who people were. He looked at how they lived in comparison to Biblical teaching. He taught the way of God in accordance with the truth and then held himself and all others accountable to the spirit and actions of that truth. Without favoritism or fear and without being influenced by their knowledge or past accomplishments, he challenged the least to the greatest to examine their current practice of the ways of God. Perhaps most impressively, he first held *himself* accountable—and then called others to follow him.

From world sector leaders to the newest Christians, from elders and evangelists to the oldest disciples in every region, we must practice the ways of God in accordance with the truth. Hypocrisy among leaders has always resulted in God bringing them down and raising up others who valued principle over position. Paul challenged Peter, the older apostle and designated holder of the keys to the kingdom, when Peter was "not acting in line with the truth of the gospel" (Galatians 2:14). God is no respecter of persons or positions when it comes to personal righteousness, as seen in the Biblical examples of kings and sons of kings (like Saul and Absalom), apostles in training (like Judas) or wealthy married couples (like Ananias and Sapphira—Acts 5). If he can raise up children for Abraham from the stones (Matthew 3:9), he will certainly raise up new leaders if the current ones do not live by his standards.

I have seen many leaders among us fall during the thirty years that I have been a disciple. In each case, two things have been obvious. First, personal righteousness was not valued and pursued in all areas of life, as often indicated by resistance to the input and accountability of others. Second, there has always been someone available to be raised up to replace the person, no matter what the person's role or profile was. As my friend Cecil Wooten used to essentially say, none of us is indispensable—and to believe otherwise invites pride over humility, God's discipline over his blessing.

Team Leadership

> Then the apostles and elders, with the whole church, decided to choose some of their own men and send them to Antioch with Paul and Barnabas. They chose Judas (called Barsabbas) and Silas, two men who were leaders among the brothers. With them they sent the following letter:
>
> The apostles and elders, your brothers,
>
> To the Gentile believers in Antioch, Syria and Cilicia:
>
> Greetings. (Acts 15:22-23)

Leadership by a single evangelist over a newly established church is certainly the pattern of church plantings and their explosive evangelistic growth as seen in the book of Acts and 1 and 2 Timothy and Titus. However, we also find in these writings Paul's instructions to appoint elders to oversee and manage God's household as it matures and ages. We could make the case that evangelists in the early church were instigators and delivery experts at the birth and infancy of new churches, but groups of greater maturity and corporate strength were the norm for long-term growth and development.

Acts 6 and 15 are examples of how both church and kingdom leadership and management quickly moved to a *group* of qualified leaders meeting needs and making decisions regarding what was best for the corporate growth of a church and the churches. The Ephesian elders (Acts 20) were to use Paul's example as a frame of reference, but they became the leadership team responsible for the continued maturing of the flock upon his departure. This pattern was to be repeated by Timothy and Titus throughout the church plantings Paul had initiated. Groups of leaders can handle more in terms of size, complexity, pressure and objectivity.

God used individuals to initiate movements, but not to single-handedly run them. The apostles clearly combined their leadership of the early Christian movement with the leadership of a group of elders (Acts 15). There seems to have been a collective wisdom hammered out by the leaders through discussions and prayer. The needs of the people, and even the voice of the people, were considered but not catered to in matters of doctrine and practice. Unity was valued over individual rights, but individual liberty was protected whenever possible. Leadership was respected and submitted to, but not feared or venerated, as had been the case with the Pharisees and Jewish religious leaders. Peter commented on Paul's work and Paul on Peter's with affection or correction, depending on what was needed. Paul respected Peter, James and John, but did not fear them or shrink back from calling for change when needed (Galatians 2). Peter did not resent Paul after being challenged, but affectionately speaks of him in 2 Peter 3:15-16 (though pointing out that some of his letters are hard to understand). Respect, but not fear, was again demonstrated.

Biblical church leaders were both humble and honest with and about one another. They were a team who needed, valued and loved one another, while never assuming that any one of them could have all the answers or could always be right. Even the dispute between Paul and Barnabas, which was later reconciled, indicates that the kingdom and its leaders were humble enough to disagree honestly and still value and leave the door open to one another through time. They divided the world in terms of ministry to Jews or Gentiles, but do not seem to have had a competitive edge toward their tasks. Instead, they displayed affection and companionship. It is troubling when we compare ourselves to, compete with and condemn other leaders with our own numbers or accomplishments. This tends to lead to dread and fear of each other in those times when we most need grace, unconditional love and support to get back on our feet and into the battle. It is far more Biblical for us to understand and to assume the best about each other in times of difficulty in our respective fields of ministry. We must do to others as we would have them do to us.

Heart and Humility

> But the Lord said to Samuel, "Do not consider his appearance or his height, for I have rejected him. The Lord does not look at the things man looks at. Man looks at the outward appearance, but the Lord looks at the heart." (1 Samuel 16:7)

The selection of Israel's first king provides further insight into what God values in leadership. He chooses differently than we naturally would think and choose. "Man looks at the outward appearance, but the Lord looks at the heart" is still as true in the twenty-first century as it was when David was selected. God can make up for lack of talent, but not for lack of heart. Appearances can be deceiving, but purity of heart will ultimately keep God's favor and divert his wrath. Saul relied on his appearance and position, and God rejected him because of his worldly attitudes and ways of leading. True spirituality enabled David to endure as God's leader through successes and failures. He was known as much for his ability to repent as for his ability to produce victory. The mighty men in his circle were greater than he was in many areas of life and battle, but they loved him with a loyalty inspired by his manner of openness, vulnerability and honesty.

Jesus was David's descendant, not only physically, but by virtue of his magnitude of spirit and love for those whom he led. Jesus took David's leadership style and reputation of being a man after God's own heart to new levels of unconditional love, commitment and self-sacrifice. He was known, like David the shepherd king, for being lowly and humble in heart. "He had no beauty or majesty to attract us to him, nothing in his appearance that we should desire him" (Isaiah 53:2). Also, "he was a man of sorrows, and acquainted with grief" (Isaiah 53:3 KJV), not a celebrity or beautiful person admired by the world. While each of us should strive to be the best we can be to the glory of God, we must stay more in touch with the common man than with the rich and famous.

Abraham Lincoln once said that God must have loved the common man because he made so many of them. Lincoln was a people's president who valued what was best for all men over what was best for only the privileged or wealthy. Church leaders must stay in touch with the grass-roots, the salt of the earth and the poor in spirit, while also converting the relatively few humble souls who are well-to-do or opinion leaders. Too often we have exalted appearance, athletics, academics and affluence when we look for leaders and when we define success in the kingdom. We need to return to purity of heart, clear consciences and sincere faith as the ultimate goals of character success in our ministries (1 Timothy 1:5).

The Desperate Need

We desperately need godly leaders. Among teens, college students, single adults and married couples with or without children, God wants to raise up leaders to motivate, train and inspire his people to be faithful, fruitful and happy. Hopefully, this book has better defined the kind of leaders God wants to raise up in terms of how we lead and treat his people. God opposes the proud, but gives grace to the humble (James 4:6; 1 Peter 5:5). He has had and will always have a people of his own for whom he defines righteousness. Our job is to aim for that righteousness in heart and character, realizing that we do not determine the times, places or positions we occupy. We can only determine the content of our heart and character, making ourselves available to be used by the Master.

Ultimately, the greatest role in the kingdom, Jesus said, is to be a servant. Servant leaders do not lord it over those whom they lead, nor do they exercise authority to get them to take action (Matthew 20:25-28). This is worldly leadership. Servants are humble; they do not claim rights or have attitudes toward the roles they are assigned. When we are servants, God can move us up, down or wherever he needs us in his service.

I have worn many hats in the kingdom, from campus minister to pulpit preacher, from evangelist/elder to geographic HOPE leader, from congregational elder to world sector elder. I can honestly say that for the last ten years, I have not sought my roles or titles; they have come to me. And I have struggled with whether I wanted them both before and after receiving them. I have concluded that God determines the times, places and positions he wants us in. I would also add that God often uses those who know us best and can see the kingdom needs from an overview perspective. Often our own ambition, biases, fears and comfort levels cause us to resist what God knows is best for us and those we could best serve. Others can often better see what we are uniquely qualified to do and what others might be able to do better than we can. The best road I can take is simply to do to others as I would like them to do to me. And who knows—the next time our roles may be reversed!

The best motto I can find for leaders is one expressed—rather amazingly—by King Nebuchadnezzar. He spoke these words after he was demoted to the least of men and then exalted to the greatest of men by God:

At the end of that time, I, Nebuchadnezzar, raised my eyes toward heaven, and my sanity was restored. Then I praised the Most High; I honored and glorified him who lives forever.

His dominion is an eternal dominion;
  his kingdom endures from generation to generation.
All the peoples of the earth
  are regarded as nothing.
He does as he pleases
  with the powers of heaven
  and the peoples of the earth.
No one can hold back his hand
  or say to him: "What have you done?"

...Now I, Nebuchadnezzar, praise and exalt and glorify the King of heaven, because everything he does is right and all his ways are just. And those who walk in pride he is able to humble. (Daniel 4:34-35, 37)

Therefore, do to others as you would have them do to you!

From Russia with Love
By Andy Fleming

I would personally like to thank Gordon and Wyndham for taking the time to write this very timely book—it is truly a labor prompted by love. As I read through the manuscript, I was reminded of one of Paul's final admonitions to the church in Colosse, "Tell Archippus: 'See to it that you complete the work you have received in the Lord'" (Colossians 4:17). Paul's public instruction to the Colossian church concerning Archippus must have produced an interesting dynamic: the disciples became personally involved in encouraging their leader to fulfill his ministry. Apparently their support was needed for Archippus to be strong in his resolve to persevere and serve diligently to the end.

Through Biblical directive and personal experience, Gordon and Wyndham have set forth some great principles of how to more effectively and righteously lead God's people. The underlying rule is simple: "Do to others as you would have them do to you" (Luke 6:31). It is right and good that every disciple has a clear expectation of love and respect from their leaders, and all of us need to be reminded that the ministry is a gift from God that needs to be fulfilled according to his divine standards. I stand amazed at the richness of God's grace and the many blessings that he bestowed on my wife, Tammy, and me during our thirteen years on the foreign mission field. I am also thankful for this opportunity to share some experiences of how I saw many of the principles described in this book prove true and bear fruit. Without a doubt Golden Rule leadership can create a more encouraging atmosphere for the whole church, as well as improve the effectiveness of leaders in serving God's people. "Let us therefore make every effort to do what leads to peace and to mutual edification" (Romans 14:19).

Learning to Listen

My wife and I were foreigners to both the culture and the language of Sweden and later Russia, where we worked as missionaries. This forced us to become students of others' ways of life before we really could become effective teachers and disciplers. Without a thorough knowledge of the people, their values, their worldview and feelings, it would have been almost impossible to lead the new converts on to maturity, due to the sense of distance and separation. As Paul said, "I have become all things to all men so that by all possible means I might save some" (1 Corinthians 9:22). In this situation, the only thing worse than assuming that I understood the people, would have been to have assumed that they understood me—such assumptions almost always proved to be damaging to growth or building deeper relationships.

As vital as this principle can be culturally speaking, it is even more important in the spiritual realm: We must understand the needs of God's people if we are going to address them properly. "He who answers before listening—that is his folly and his shame" (Proverbs 18:13). People neither need nor want pat answers and generic teaching; they desire to be understood and clearly shown the way by example. If we are going to minister effectively, we must be in touch with what the disciples are feeling and fully aware of the issues that they are facing in their day-to-day situations.

At some point during the first year of our ministry in Moscow, I began to hold an open quiet time at our home at 6:30 AM on Friday mornings for any of the brothers who wanted to come. The format was simple with hot tea, coffee and cookies, an hour of individual Bible study and then a half an hour of sharing and prayer. Although the first few meetings were initiated in response to the requests of brothers simply wanting to have better devotional times with God, it didn't take long to see that this was an incredible opportunity to get a sense of how things were really going in the membership of the church. This Friday morning quiet time became a tradition in the Fleming household, and for the next eight years it was as fixed in my weekly schedule as our Sunday worship service. Sometimes more than twenty brothers would show up, and as the church in Moscow approached three thousand in membership, their friendship and openness often supplied me with ideas and insights about what the church needed to be taught and areas in which the ministry staff needed to be trained.

Another meeting that was not quite as encouraging but equally as useful for guiding the Moscow church was my Saturday morning "Bad Attitude Fellowship." Fairly regularly, I would pick a Saturday morning to host a two- to three-hour meeting for regular members suffering with critical attitudes toward the leadership or toward the church in general. Whenever I heard of discontent or disagreements within the church that sounded serious (in need of more mature leadership to bring resolution), I would invite the involved parties over for a Saturday morning meeting. Although some of these meetings were occasionally necessary for dealing with false teaching—or even false teachers—that had somehow found its way into the fellowship, much more often it was cases of unresolved conflict between disciples or even specifically between disciples and their Bible talk leaders or ministry staff. Thankfully, it was not the same group of people at every meeting, and in most cases resolution came within a few hours. Again, many of the issues that surfaced in these meetings were incredibly valuable in the teaching and training of the disciples throughout the whole congregation.

Shared Decision-Making

One of the practical challenges in planting a church in a third world economy is understanding the amazing difference in experience between those of us raised in the relative wealth of the first world and those brothers and sisters brought up in much more austere financial conditions. The balance between not spoiling the nationals on staff with too much financial support and creating resentment by not supplying them with adequate support required the wisdom of Solomon. Therefore, I turned to the book of Proverbs for a solution: "Plans fail for lack of counsel, but with many advisers they succeed" (Proverbs 15:22).

In the fall of 1996, I called together the regional shepherding couples who were responsible for helping with the spiritually weak brothers and sisters in their regions and asked them to help come up with a salary model for the staff members of the Moscow church. All these couples were working secular jobs, some of them being middle-aged with teenage children. After discussing the various components of such a model and the specific needs of the ministry staff, these ten couples decided on a proposal that actually paid the ministry couples at a higher level than eight of the ten couples involved in the discussion. In addition the majority thought that the sector leaders should also be equipped with pagers to make them more accessible to the members of their respective groups—a definite trademark of the small but ever-growing middle class beginning to emerge in Russia that I had hesitated to promote due to its "first worldness." I was amazed, relieved and very encouraged by their leadership and decisions.

The benefits of using this consensus approach were undeniable: (1) the solution was functional and fair, since it was produced by mature people of that society who received no direct benefit from the model (except maybe gratefulness on the part of the ministry staff); (2) as the lead evangelist, I was protected from my own sentimentality and limitations; and (3) the regional shepherds felt respected and useful. Thanks be to God for many advisers and great advice!

'Leadership' Culture Shock

The long-term viability of a church planting on foreign soil that is initially led and staffed by missionaries is totally based on their ability to involve the local converts in the building process and to eventually train them to lead. If the indigenous peoples' voice is not heard, the church will become unrelatable and suspect to the native population, and growth will become very difficult. Sadly, we often do not recognize that within every group (foreign or domestic), there is a tendency to produce a leadership subculture that can also lose touch with mainstream thought and concern. Parallel to the example of an estranged American church planting on foreign soil, first-world leadership that is overly concerned with its own needs can become unrelatable and suspect to the general membership. Fortunately for us, Jesus presented us with a simple solution for such a predicament: servant leadership.

Although a fairly typical American attitude toward leadership is that "Everyone wants to be the leader" and a fairly typical Russian attitude is that "No one wants to be the leader," the challenge of Jesus remains the same: "Whoever wants to become great among you must be your servant" (Mark 10:43). In this same passage Jesus identified himself as the "slave of all," but this did not reduce him in any way to a mindless slave controlled by the whim of every human being with whom he came in contact. Ephesians 5:21-33 teaches us that as a husband submits to the needs of his wife (her needs define the decisions he should make), Jesus submitted himself to the whole human race, allowing our needs to define the decisions he made. Jesus exemplified Paul's admonition of Philippians 2:3: "Do nothing out of selfish ambition or vain conceit, but in humility consider others better than yourselves." The plans and directions of Christlike leadership are defined by the needs of the church. All leadership roles are established by him in order to:

> ...prepare God's people for works of service, so that the body
> of Christ may be built up until we all reach unity in the faith
> and in the knowledge of the Son of God and become mature,
> attaining to the whole measure of the fullness of Christ.
> (Ephesians 4:12-13)

The goal of having human leadership roles in the church is not simply for a few people to do the work of the ministry, but for the whole church to be built up and trained for the work of the ministry.

Building Others Up

I can never thank God enough for the privilege of preaching the gospel to the spiritually starved souls of Russia back in 1991. Their openness and response was truly incredible. Every member of the original team, most of whom had not yet even begun to learn the language until we moved to Moscow, will testify that the Russians simply "turned themselves in" as we opened the Bible with them, showed them God's plan of salvation through Jesus Christ and shared our lives with them. Of course, a great number of baptisms is only one component of great church growth—teaching disciples to obey the commandments of Jesus, as well as encouraging and strengthening their faith, is a lifelong process.

I am so appreciative of the priority that Gordon and Wyndham demonstrated by devoting an entire chapter of this book to focus on teaching the Bible. It is much too easy to replace the Holy Spirit and God's word in our discipling of one another with human emotion and opinion, which is superficially similar, but produces vastly different results. The minister of God's word has been given the responsibility of being both a spiritual dietitian and master chef, preparing hearty and wholesome meals for God's people. For me one of the most rewarding duties of being a minister is to evaluate the need, prepare a lesson and encourage transformation through the public proclamation of the God's word. During our eight years in Russia, I wrote and delivered more than 600 different lessons and also did not hesitate to repeat them if similar circumstances arose again. As I look back over my lesson files, the titles are like diary entries describing the particular needs and struggles in the life of the church during those times. Every time we would face a new obstacle or hit a new wall, God was giving us the opportunity to obtain greater insight and deeper understanding into his power, character and will. I am also eternally grateful for the discipling and training that we received from the Kip McKeans and Fuquas while we were in Moscow, since God also used them to teach us many important lessons from the Scriptures, both for ourselves and for the church.

Finally...

When an expert in the law asked Jesus what was the greatest commandment in the Law, Jesus answered:

> "'Love the Lord your God with all your heart and with all your soul and with all your mind.' This is the first and greatest commandment. And the second is like it: 'Love your neighbor as yourself.'" (Matthew 22:37-39)

Truly the Golden Rule is just another way of saying, "Love your neighbor as yourself." God commands it and everyone benefits when it is obeyed. Every disciple wants to have their needs met, their hearts understood, their weaknesses strengthened and their dreams encouraged. Leading by the Golden Rule ensures the right attitude in leadership to fulfill all of these expectations. Leading by the Golden Rule ensures God's blessing.

Who Are We?

Discipleship Publications International (DPI) began publishing in 1993. We are a nonprofit Christian publisher affiliated with the International Churches of Christ, committed to publishing and distributing materials that honor God, lift up Jesus Christ and show how his message practically applies to all areas of life. We have a deep conviction that no one changes life like Jesus and that the implementation of his teaching will revolutionize any life, any marriage, any family and any singles household.

Since our beginning, we have published more than 110 titles; plus, we have produced a number of important, spiritual audio products. More than one million volumes have been printed, and our works have been translated into more than a dozen languages—international is not just a part of our name! Our books are shipped regularly to every inhabited continent.

To see a more detailed description of our works, find us on the World Wide Web at www.dpibooks.org. You can order books by calling 1-888-DPI-BOOK twenty-four hours a day. From outside the U.S., call 978-670-8840 ext. 227 during Boston-area business hours.

We appreciate the hundreds of comments we have received from readers. We would love to hear from you. Here are other ways to get in touch:

Mail: DPI, 2 Sterling Road, Billerica, Mass. 01862-2595
E-Mail: dpibooks@icoc.org

Find Us on the
World Wide Web

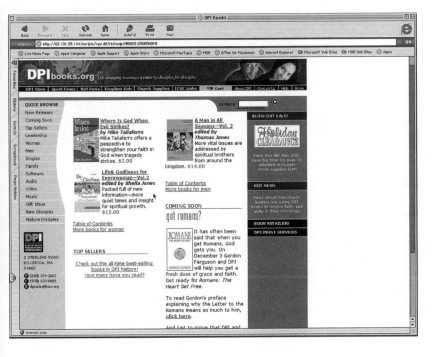

www.dpibooks.org
1-888-DPI-BOOK
outside the US:
978-670-8840 ext. 227